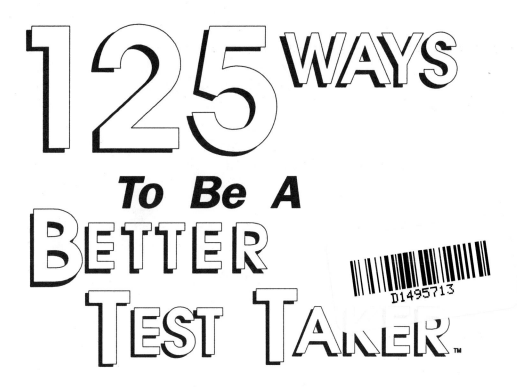

125 WAYS
To Be A
BETTER TEST TAKER™

A Program for Test Success

Andrea M. Lazzari
Judy W. Wood

Skill Area:	Assessment
Ages:	12-18

LinguiSystems

LinguiSystems, Inc.
3100 4th Avenue
East Moline, IL 61244

1-800-PRO IDEA
1-800-776-4332

Printed in the U.S.A.
ISBN 1-55999-417-7

About the Authors

Andrea M. Lazzari

Judy W. Wood

Andrea M. Lazzari, Ed.D., is an assistant professor of special education at Virginia Commonwealth University in Richmond, Virginia. She has worked as a speech-language pathologist in the public schools, in a community clinic, and in private practice. She has also been a teacher of preschool students with disabilities and the Supervisor of Early Childhood Special Education Programs for the state of Virginia. *125 Ways to Be a Better Test Taker* is Andrea's sixteenth publication with LinguiSystems.

Judy W. Wood, Ph.D., is a professor of special education at Virginia Commonwealth University in Richmond, Virginia. She received her bachelor's degree in English and Mental Retardation, and her master's and Ph.D. degrees in Special Education from the University of Southern Mississippi in Hattiesburg. She taught English and special education classes in the public schools while she was working on her graduate degrees. Judy conducts in-service workshops for general and special education teachers throughout the United States. *125 Ways to Be a Better Test Taker* is Judy's first publication with LinguiSystems.

January 1994

Acknowledgement

Our thanks are extended to Sara Tilley, Jennifer Darragh, and Tracy Baird for their help in typing and editing rough drafts of this manuscript.

Dedication

To our colleagues across the country—for their willingness to share their ideas and skills with us, and for their enthusiastic support of our efforts!

Table of Contents

Outline

12 Ways to Study for a Test

    1   Make a list of the information that will be covered.

    2   Write down what will not be covered on the test.

    3   Ask what types of questions will be on the test.

    4   Prepare study aids based on question types.

    5   Ask if a study guide is available.

    6   Check your notebook for complete notes.

    7   Ask questions about anything in your notes that's unclear.

    8   Highlight important information in your notes.

    9   Practice putting ideas from class in your own words.

   10   Mark possible test questions in the margins of your notes.

   11   Use more than one channel to learn the information.

   12   Break up material you're studying into smaller sections.

10 Ways to Prepare for a Test

   13   Get to class early.

   14   Choose a location in the class with few distractions.

   15   Get all your test materials ready.

   16   Review the highlighted parts of your notes.

   17   Avoid discussing the test with your classmates.

   18   Look over the entire test before answering any questions.

   19   Read the directions carefully and underline cue words.

   20   Ask your teacher to explain any unclear directions.

   21   Answer the easy questions first.

   22   Work at your own pace.

4 Ways to Read and Understand Directions

   23   Read each direction twice.

   24   Find the key words or phrases.

   25   Make sure you understand the key words or phrases.

   26   Mark through irrelevant information with your pencil.

15 Ways to Answer True/False Questions

27   Read each statement carefully.

28   Underline important cue words.

29   Follow directions for marking your answers.

30   Mark your answers without looking for a pattern.

31   Write clearly.

32   Answer the easiest questions first.

33   Look at the entire statement.

34   Look for exceptions to a statement.

35   Focus on the question you're answering.

36   Look for cue words often used in FALSE questions.

37   Look for cue words often used in TRUE questions.

38   Identify double negatives in statements.

39   Identify negative words and negative prefixes in statements.

40   Guess at questions you're unsure of.

41   Keep your original answer, unless you're sure it's wrong.

19 Ways to Answer Multiple Choice Questions

42   Identify the two parts of multiple choice questions.

43   Identify the type of question you're answering.

44   Decide if you're looking for the *correct* answer or the *best* answer.

45   Try to answer the question before looking at the choices.

46   Read all the choices before marking your answer.

47   Try each choice in the blank.

48   Answer the questions you know first.

49   Look carefully for distractors.

50   Identify cue words often used with incorrect choices.

51   Draw a line through incorrect choices.

52   Identify cue words often used with correct choices.

53   Write a brief rationale for choosing an answer.

54   Use other questions as clues.

55 Follow grammar rules as possible clues to answers.

56 Choose "All of the above" if you're unsure of the answer.

57 Read each choice with the stem.

58 Answer all of the questions.

59 Check your work.

60 Have faith in yourself.

10 Ways to Answer Matching Questions

61 Ask if there's a penalty for incorrect answers.

62 Read the directions carefully.

63 Read all the items in both columns before you begin to answer.

64 Match the items you know first.

65 Start with the first item in the first column.

66 Draw a line through answers you've used.

67 Begin with the column with the longest choices.

68 Narrow down the choices.

69 See how many choices are in each column.

70 Check the part of speech when matching synonyms.

12 Ways to Answer Completion Questions

71 Ask if a word bank will be provided on the test.

72 Look at the length of the blank.

73 Look at the number of blanks.

74 Try to complete the answer without looking at the word bank.

75 Cross off choices in the word bank as you use them.

76 Answer remaining items with unused words from the word bank.

77 Answer each sentence separately when completing a paragraph.

78 Check to see if the answer is grammatically correct.

79 Check the word right before the blank.

80 Answer as close to the correct answer as possible when guessing.

81 Answer all of the questions.

82 Guess if you have to—you may get partial credit.

21 Ways to Answer Definition Questions

83 Practice a 3-step approach to learning definitions.

84 Use flash cards to study.

85 Use a memory strategy for remembering words and definitions.

86 Study words and definitions in groups of five.

87 Find a study partner.

88 Vary the study technique you use with your partner.

89 Think of short definitions for words.

90 Highlight prefixes, suffixes, and root words.

91 Learn basic root words.

92 Learn prefix meanings.

93 Learn suffix meanings.

94 Use visualization and association to help recall definitions.

95 Make up jingles to help you learn definitions.

96 Look for small words within words.

97 Match your study technique to the type of test.

98 Complete the definitions you know first.

99 Use the number and length of blanks as a clue to the answer.

100 Look for "a" or "an" right before the blank.

101 Decide which part of speech is missing from an incomplete sentence.

102 Use context clues.

103 Take a chance.

7 Ways to Answer Reading Comprehension Questions

104 Read the passage over quickly.

105 Read the passage a second time.

106 Try to answer multiple choice questions by looking at the stem only.

107 Look back at the passage if you're unsure of the answer.

108 Look for the main idea.

109 Back up your answer with an explanation or a reason.

110 Double-check your answers.

15 Ways to Answer Essay Questions

    111 Read the prompt.

    112 Reread the prompt.

    113 Find and underline the command word.

    114 Define the command word.

    115 Determine the category or purpose of the command word.

    116 Change a question into a statement with a command word.

    117 Decide if your answer can be completed in one paragraph.

    118 Form a topic sentence.

    119 Write the main idea.

    120 Add details to your main idea.

    121 Use the main idea and details to develop a visual organizer.

    122 Check the time remaining to answer the question.

    123 Complete your answer in a written format.

    124 Close your essay with a summary statement.

    125 Read your essay to make sure it's complete.

Introduction

Mastering the skill of testing is difficult for many students, especially for students with language-learning disorders. Students at-risk or students with disabilities, particularly those with language disorders, learning disabilities, or mild mental retardation are especially challenged by a written test format. Many times this isn't because they haven't studied or don't understand the material, but it's because they don't understand the test directions or format. *125 Ways to Be a Better Test Taker* is designed to meet the needs of such students.

Much of the information published on testing is directed toward the teachers rather than toward the students. Unfortunately, this information doesn't always filter down to the students. *125 Ways to Be a Better Test Taker* provides helpful information for you and your students to use in these eight areas of testing.

- ❑ Reading and Understanding Directions

- ❑ True/False Statements

- ❑ Multiple Choice Questions

- ❑ Matching Questions

- ❑ Completion Questions

- ❑ Definition Questions

- ❑ Reading Comprehension Questions

- ❑ Essay Questions

Each unit begins with a teacher Overview and a brief description of the student Focus, Handout, and Activity Sheets. The body of each unit contains a student Focus to explain the importance of each question type, one or more Handouts that give test tips, Activity Sheets designed to target specific test skills, and a Practice Test to assess progress. This book also includes an Answer Key for the practice items and tests, and an Appendix with general teacher tips for better test results.

Although we couldn't give examples of every question type in the context of each curricular area, we've attempted to cover a variety of curricular areas in the activity sheets. Most of the practice items were written with a relatively low level of difficulty so your students could focus on the test skill or strategy presented without becoming frustrated with difficult or new content. At the same time, we felt it important to include practice items with a language level appropriate for middle- and secondary-level students.

As your students progress through *125 Ways to Be a Better Test Taker*, we suggest you note which types of questions seem the most difficult for them. Then, work with their classroom teachers to obtain additional practice items that directly represent classroom content. This will allow your students to practice with relevant curricular material.

Research has shown that good test-taking skills are a leading factor in promoting school success. In addition, studies have shown that direct instruction in test-taking skills has resulted in significant gains among groups of pupils as well as individual students. *125 Ways to Be a Better Test Taker* has been developed to provide your students with opportunities for direct practice that lead to test success. As you progress through the units in this book, you'll see your students' confidence levels rise as they learn strategies for becoming test-wise!

Andrea and Judy

Unit 1: General Test-Taking Skills

Overview

You probably know of several students that perform poorly on tests regardless of the number of hours they spend studying. Students who are test-wise know that preparing for a test involves more than reading the material and memorizing the facts. In fact, strategies for good test performance center around having strong study skills, being prepared on test day, and reading and understanding test directions.

This unit will guide your students through tips and practice items that help them prepare for tests. The tips on the handouts are intended to relieve test anxiety and help your students gain some control over the testing situation. They'll also help your students enter the room with a positive attitude and feel relaxed and confident about the test.

In this unit, your students will learn the following strategies to become more proficient at preparing for tests.

❒ Recognizing the importance of preparing for a test.

❒ Organizing their notes and study materials to make the most use of their study time.

❒ Becoming aware of things they can do prior to receiving their test papers.

❒ Understanding how reading and following directions affect test performance.

❒ Identifying key words and phrases and irrelevant information in directions.

You can help your students learn and succeed by preparing them for tests. The teacher tips below give you information to consider before giving a test.

Teacher Tips for Preparing Students

Conduct in-class reviews using sample questions.

Set aside time in class for small groups of students to quiz one another.

Provide study guides that specify the key points and location of information to study.

Provide word banks, review questions, sample test questions, outlines of major topics, etc. as study aids.

Give a description of the test in terms of the length, number, and types of items.

Focus

General Test-Taking Skills *(page 14)*

The focus will help your students understand the importance of tests. Explain your rationale for giving tests and why you spend so much time preparing and grading them. Then, read and discuss the focus. Talk about the importance of having good study skills, preparing yourself on test day, and reading and understanding the test directions.

Handouts

12 Ways to Study for a Test *(page 15)*

Improving your students' study skills is the focus of this handout. Your students learn valuable strategies for helping them organize their notes and other test information, prepare study aids, and practice putting ideas from class into their own words.

10 Ways to Prepare for a Test *(page 17)*

Your students probably put little thought into what things they'll need to do on test day to prepare for a test—things like getting to class early and having enough sharpened pencils on hand. This handout serves as an excellent checklist for students on test day.

4 Ways to Read and Understand Directions *(page 19)*

Students who know and understand the material presented in class may perform poorly on tests because they don't understand the test directions. You'll see test scores improve as your students learn these success strategies for reading and following directions.

Activity Sheets

Key Words and Phrases *(page 20)*

All directions contain key words or phrases that tell your students what to do. These key words and phrases give students specific directions that tell them how to answer questions.

In this activity, your students learn that the first step in taking a test is to read the directions and find the key words or phrases.

Know Your Stuff *(page 21)*

Students who have difficulty understanding and following directions won't perform well on tests, even if they know the material. If your students aren't sure they understand the directions on a test, encourage them to answer one question and then ask you if they've correctly followed the directions.

This activity gives your students practice writing key phrases in their own words.

Cross It Out *(page 22)*

Identifying irrelevant or distracting information in test directions is an important skill. In this activity, encourage your students to look for the key words or phrases before lightly marking through the extra information.

Practice Test

Give your students the practice test as a pretest to this unit and as a posttest to assess their progress relating to general test-taking skills. Encourage your students to use the handouts from this unit to help them with the posttest.

Focus: General Test-Taking Skills

"Why do we have to take tests?"

"Teachers love to give hard tests!"

"I never get good grades on tests—even when I study!"

Have you ever had any of these thoughts? If so, you're not alone! Most students have never liked taking tests. But it may surprise you to know that many teachers don't like giving tests any more than students like taking them.

So why do teachers keep giving tests? One reason is because tests are one way to see how much you've learned. They tell you and your teacher if you've learned the material presented in class. Are you ready to move on to new information, or do you need to continue studying the same material?

For example, when you're playing a video game, you need to learn the functions of the keys before you can play the game. And as you're playing, many times you need to master one skill or level before you can move on to the next one. When you were younger, you had to know how to add fractions before you could learn how to multiply them. Your math teacher probably gave you a test to see if you were ready to learn how to multiply fractions.

Sometimes you won't do well on a test even if you've studied for hours. No matter how long you study, though, you won't get good test scores if your notes are thrown together or if you're not sure what the test covers or what the test directions mean.

This unit will help you focus on ways to study for a test, to prepare yourself on test day, and to read the test directions. After you complete this unit, you'll be more relaxed and confident about tests. You'll be off to a great start at improving your test scores!

12 Ways to Study for a Test

Studying for a test involves more than reading the material and memorizing important facts. Here are 12 study tips to help you improve your test scores!

1   **Make a list of the information that will be covered.**

Ask your teacher what the test will cover. Write down the chapter, page numbers, and the main topics so you'll be sure to study the right material.

2   **Write down what will not be covered on the test.**

Ask your teacher what information won't be covered on the test. Write down this information, too, so you'll know what you don't need to study.

3   **Ask what types of questions will be on the test.**

Will the test be mostly true/false statements or matching items? Will there be any essay questions? Ask your teacher what kinds of questions you can expect so you get an idea of how to study for the test.

4   **Prepare study aids based on question types.**

After your teacher tells you what kinds of questions to expect on the test, make flash cards or other study aids based on the kinds of questions you'll be answering. For example, if you know there'll be definitions on the test, write each **boldfaced** or *italicized* term from your textbook on one side of an index card. Then, write the definitions on the backs of the cards and use them to study.

5   **Ask if a study guide is available.**

Some teachers are happy to provide a study guide. When you're getting ready to study for a test, ask your teacher if there's a study guide you can use.

6   **Check your notebook for complete notes.**

Look through your notes before studying for a test to make sure you're not missing any information. You may even want to compare your notes with a classmate's to see if you have all the notes you need.

7 **Ask questions about anything in your notes that's unclear.**

As you read over your notes, put a question mark next to anything that doesn't make sense. You'll want to ask your teacher as soon as you can to explain anything you don't understand. Don't wait until the day before the test to do this—it'll be too late to ask for help.

8 **Highlight important information in your notes.**

Read over your notes and highlight important information, like facts, dates, names, and places. For easy identification, use a different color highlighter for each category. For example, highlight names in blue, dates in yellow, and places in pink.

9 **Practice putting ideas from class in your own words.**

As you're studying, practice defining terms and words and explaining major themes and ideas without looking at your notes. It'll be easier to remember the information if you practice repeating the major points from class in your own words.

10 **Mark possible test questions in the margins of your notes.**

What questions would you ask if you were the teacher? As you're reviewing your notes, make notes of possible test questions. Make sure you can answer these questions!

11 **Use more than one channel to learn the information.**

Try a different study routine to help you remember information. Instead of silently reading the information, try reading it out loud. You can also practice saying the answers out loud or writing the information as you try to memorize it.

12 **Break up material you're studying into smaller sections.**

The purpose of studying is to learn the material so you remember it, not just to memorize it long enough to take the test. You'll learn material better if you break it into small sections. For example, if you have 20 vocabulary words to learn, work on five each night for four nights. Then, spend the night before the test reviewing all 20 words. Don't wait until the night before a test to learn new material.

10 Ways to Prepare for a Test

There are several things you can do on the day of a test to guarantee your success. The ten tips below are a good checklist to follow on test day.

13   Get to class early.

You'll do better on the test if you give yourself time to choose a seat, relax, and get ready to take the test.

14   Choose a location in the class with few distractions.

Try to stay away from open doors or windows where you'll be easily distracted. Choose a seat where you'll be able to focus on the test.

15   Get all your test materials ready.

Before the test begins, make sure you have extra sharpened pencils, an eraser, a calculator, a ruler, or any supplies you'll need so you don't have to worry during the test.

16   Review the highlighted parts of your notes.

Spend 5-10 minutes looking over the highlighted parts of your notes. This will be a quick reminder of important information and get your brain thinking about the topic the test covers.

17   Avoid discussing the test with your classmates.

Don't expect to earn a good grade by relying on information your classmates give you about the test—they might be wrong.

18   Look over the entire test before answering any questions.

Quickly read all of the directions, and decide how long you'll spend on each section.

19   Read the directions carefully and underline cue words.

It's important to do exactly what the directions tell you. Even if you know the answer to a question, you may not get points for your answer if you haven't followed the directions.

10 Ways to Prepare for a Test, *continued*

20 **Ask your teacher to explain any unclear directions.**

Don't be embarrassed to ask your teacher for an explanation of directions or words you don't understand. You won't lose points for asking a question—so always ask, unless your teacher tells you she won't answer any questions about the test.

21 **Answer the easy questions first.**

Don't panic if the test seems hard when you first look at it. Answer the questions you know first. As you continue working, you'll discover that you know more than you thought you did!

22 **Work at your own pace.**

Don't rush to turn in your paper when everyone else does. The first paper turned in may not be the best one—the last paper turned in could be the "A" paper!

4 Ways to Read and Understand Directions

It's difficult to answer questions correctly if you don't understand the test directions. Here are four tips to get you on the right track.

23   **Read each direction twice.**

Read each direction carefully before beginning the test. Don't just skim over it, read it word for word. Then, read the direction again.

24   **Find the key words or phrases.**

All directions have key words or phrases that tell you exactly what to do. These key words and phrases give you specific directions that tell you how to answer the questions. The first step in taking a test is to read the directions and find the key words or phrases.

25   **Make sure you understand the key words or phrases.**

It's important to know what each key word or phrase in a direction means before you begin answering the questions. If you're not sure you understand the direction, answer one question and ask your teacher if you've followed the direction correctly.

26   **Mark through irrelevant information with your pencil.**

Sometimes directions contain extra information that takes your attention away from the key words or phrases. After you've identified the key words or phrases, look for the extra information and lightly mark through it. Here's an example.

~~Below are ten definitions.~~ <u>Match each definition</u> ~~at the left with a term to the right.~~ ~~Place the letter of the correct term in the space next to its definition.~~

Key Words and Phrases

Name _____

You can lose valuable points if you don't follow the directions for answering questions.

All directions have key words or phrases that tell you exactly what to do. Underline the key words or phrases in the directions below. The first one is done for you.

1. <u>Circle the letter</u> of the best answer.

2. Choose the best answer for each question.

3. Fill in each blank below.

4. Finish each of the following sentences.

5. Put a *T* next to each true statement.

6. Draw a circle around the correct answer.

7. List the colors in a rainbow.

8. Circle the word *False* if the statement is false.

9. Answer three of the five questions below.

10. Choose the letter of the correct answer and write it on the line to the left of the statement.

11. Choose the word that best completes each sentence and write it in the blank.

12. Look at the sentences below. One of the underlined terms is incorrect. Cross out the incorrect term.

13. Match each definition on the left with a word on the right. Place the letter of the correct word on the blank before its definition.

14. Develop a paragraph or two to discuss each of the four points listed above.

Know Your Stuff

Name _____

It's important to understand what each key word or phrase means before you begin answering the questions. Make sure you know what the directions are telling you to do so you know how to answer the questions.

Write what each key phrase means in your own words on the line below it. The first one is done for you.

1. Choose the correct answer for each question below, and write the letter in the blank beside the question.

    Write the letter of the correct answer on the blank.
    _____

2. Match the words on the left to their meanings on the right by writing the correct number in each blank.

    _____

3. Proofread the following letter. Correct the mistakes.

    _____

4. To the left of each statement, write *True* if the statement is correct. If the statement is not true, write *False*.

    _____

5. Identify five sources of help for a medical emergency.

    _____

6. Develop a paragraph that summarizes your view on women serving in the military.

    _____

7. Arrange the following events in chronological order by placing a **1** beside the first event in time, etc.

    _____

8. Explain why freedom of speech is important to you. Support each of your points with a specific example.

    _____

Cross It Out

Name _____

Some directions contain extra information that takes your attention away from the key words or phrases. When this happens, first underline the key words or phrases. Then, lightly mark through the extra information so you can focus on the important directions.

Cross out the extra or irrelevant information in each set of directions below. The first one is done for you.

1. ~~Define each word.~~ Write a synonym for each word in the blank next to it.

2. Arrange these events in the correct order. Put a **1** by the event that happened first, a **2** by the event that happened second, and so on. Don't leave out any events.

3. Read the passage below. After reading the passage, answer each of the questions.

4. Write a word in the blank to complete each sentence. Fill in each blank with the best word from the word bank.

5. Match each event with its date. Write the date of the event in the blank next to it.

6. Below are ten definitions. Match each definition at the left with a term at the right. Place the letter of the correct term in the space next to its definition.

7. The map below shows the average annual rainfall in South America. After studying the map carefully, answer the questions below. You may write on the map.

8. For each statement below, choose the most appropriate response based on your knowledge of the word in italics. Indicate your choice by writing the letter on the blank to the left of the statement.

9. List the five most important questions a consumer should ask when purchasing a new refrigerator. Be sure to write your answers in the form of questions rather than statements.

10. Use each word in the list below in a complete sentence. Be sure the sentence shows the meaning of the word in context.

 **Practice Test**   Name _____

Circle the letter of the correct response.

1. If you know there will be definitions on a test you should _____ .

    a. go through your book and make a list of important words and terms

    b. go through your book and make a list of important dates

    c. spend your study time putting key terms in alphabetical order

2. A good way to study for a test is to _____ .

    a. read all the material silently a few times

    b. make up questions that might be on the test and try to answer them

    c. study terms in groups of 25 or more

3. On test day, it's best to _____ .

    a. turn in your paper when everyone else does

    b. turn in your paper first

    c. turn in your paper when you've carefully answered all the questions and checked the test

4. If a test looks hard when you first look at it, you should _____ .

    a. answer the questions you know first

    b. give up

    c. tell the teacher you can't do it

Read each statement. If it's good advice, write *good* next to it. If it's bad advice, write *bad* next to it.

5. a. _____ Try to memorize information in your own words.

    b. _____ Don't ask your teacher any questions during the test.

    c. _____ Look over your notes the night before a test to see if anything is missing.

    d. _____ If you're not sure of an answer, always guess.

    e. _____ Start the test by answering the questions you know first. Save the questions you don't know until last.

    f. _____ Don't look at the clock during a test. It'll only make you nervous.

Unit 2: True/False Statements

Overview

Teachers at all levels and across all content areas use true/false statements on tests as an objective assessment of students' knowledge and mastery of facts. The format is quick and easy to prepare, and the items are easy to grade because the answers are fairly objective.

One of the most common errors students make on true/false tests is not reading the statements carefully before responding. In this unit, your students will learn and practice the following strategies to become more proficient at answering true/false questions.

- ❏ Increasing their awareness of general techniques to use with true/false statements.

- ❏ Identifying cue words in true/false statements and knowing which ones signal TRUE or FALSE.

- ❏ Thinking of exceptions to statements to determine they're FALSE.

- ❏ Understanding that all parts of a statement must be true for it to be considered TRUE.

- ❏ Interpreting statements using negatives, double negatives, and prefixes.

You can help your students perform better on true/false tests by evaluating your method of writing items. The teacher tips give you information to consider when writing tests.

Teacher Tips for Test Construction

Write the items to the point. Students shouldn't be required to read meaning into statements or to try to think of obscure counterexamples.

Use familiar vocabulary words. Using new or difficult vocabulary assesses students' word knowledge rather than their factual knowledge of a subject area.

Use a consistent response format from one test to another.

Include a reasonable number of items on any test. 50 true/false statements can overwhelm students, especially if this format is difficult for them.

Give samples of true/false statements in your lectures and in the discussion before the test if you're going to use these items when testing.

Ask your students to generate true/false statements from the material covered in class as a review. Have them exchange items and work in groups to answer them. Let them know you'll be using some of their statements on the test.

Focus

True/False Statements *(page 28)*

How well do your students remember facts? Before introducing the focus, encourage your students to name some facts they know related to their personal lives, as well as some facts they've learned in school. Explain how knowing facts helps your students be better problem solvers and enables them to make good decisions. After your students have read the focus, ask them what facts they'd need to know to make decisions about the questions listed.

Handout

15 Ways to Answer True/False Questions *(page 29)*

This handout gives your students detailed strategies for correctly answering true/false statements. Use it as a springboard for class discussion to familiarize your students with the language of testing. Encourage them to refer to this handout before and during any test that includes true/false statements.

Activity Sheets

Cue Words *(page 32)*

Locating cue words in true/false statements helps your students identify important information. In this activity, your students practice underlining some of these cue words.

never	always	not	worst	none
every	invariably	exactly	best	all
often	bad	good	sometimes	fewer
less	some	seldom	more	most
many	usually	equal		

Cue Word Clues *(page 33)*

Cue words often give your students clues to help them answer true/false statements correctly. For example, questions are usually FALSE when they state that something is *always* TRUE. Tell your students these cue words usually indicate that a question is FALSE.

never	always	not	none	every
best	worst	exactly	all	invariably
only	first	totally	because	

More Cue Word Clues *(page 34)*

Some cue words may indicate that a true/false statement is TRUE. Help your students understand that questions are usually TRUE when they contain these cue words.

bad	occasionally	less	usually	good
more	generally	seldom	sometimes	many
may	equally	mainly	probably	fewer
most	frequently	often	might	some

It's an Exception *(page 35)*

This activity gives your students practice identifying exceptions to true/false statements. If your students can think of one exception to a statement, the question is FALSE. If they can't think of an exception to a statement, they should mark the question TRUE.

All or None *(page 36)*

Teach your students that all parts of a true/false statement must be true in order for the answer to be TRUE. If any part of a statement is false, they should mark the question FALSE. This activity gives your students practice identifying the false parts of statements.

Negative to Positive *(page 37)*

True/False statements that contain double negatives can be correctly answered when students learn this strategy.

- Underline both negative words.
- Change the negative words to positive words.
- Reread the statement.
- Choose your answer.

Tell your students that the following are some common negative words.

is not	will not	could not
isn't	won't	couldn't
do not	cannot	should not
don't	can't	shouldn't

Word Play *(page 38)*

This activity teaches your students to identify negative words and negative prefixes. Use the examples below to help your students understand that negative words and negative prefixes can change the meanings of true/false statements.

<u>Never</u> use yeast to make bread.

The boat is <u>not</u> a sailboat.

The boy is <u>inactive</u>.

It's <u>impossible</u> to climb that mountain.

Give your students this list of words with common negative prefixes. Have them look up the definitions of these words in a dictionary. How many other words can they add to this list?

<u>un</u>able	<u>in</u>accurate	<u>im</u>polite	<u>dis</u>agree	<u>ir</u>relevant
<u>un</u>certain	<u>in</u>famous	<u>im</u>perfect	<u>dis</u>continue	<u>ir</u>regular
<u>un</u>common	<u>in</u>efficient	<u>im</u>movable	<u>dis</u>approve	<u>ir</u>responsible
<u>un</u>armed	<u>in</u>flexible	<u>im</u>proper	<u>dis</u>band	<u>ir</u>rational
<u>un</u>easy	<u>in</u>excusable	<u>im</u>probable	<u>dis</u>place	<u>ir</u>resistible

Practice Test

Give your students the practice test as a pretest to this unit and as a posttest to assess their progress answering true/false statements. Encourage your students to use the handout from this unit to help them with the posttest.

Focus: True/False Statements

Many of the subjects you study in school are based on facts. For example, in science class you may learn this fact: Animals can be classified into three groups—omnivores, herbivores, and carnivores. In Social Studies your teacher may expect you to learn this fact: You must be 35 years old and a U.S. citizen to be elected President of the United States.

Facts may not be as interesting to learn as some other things, but they are important. One reason it's important to learn facts is because they provide you with accurate information to help you make good decisions and solve problems. You need to know facts to decide things like:

- Which lunch choice is the healthiest?

- What's the best boom box I can get with the money I've saved?

- What kind of clothing should I pack for a trip far from where I live?

- Where and when is this movie taking place?

Teachers use true/false statements on tests to see how well you remember facts. To answer a true/false question correctly, you need to understand the statement and know the fact. The tips and practice pages in this unit will help you understand the language of true/false statements. Once you learn the key words to look for, the mystery of true/false statements will be unlocked!

28

15 Ways to Answer True/False Questions

Answering true/false questions correctly can be tricky! Here are 15 tips to help you choose your answers.

27 Read each statement carefully.

It's important to read each statement carefully—sometimes one word can change the meaning of the statement. If you're unsure of the answer, take time to read the statement a second time before answering the question.

28 Underline important cue words.

Cue words are words that give you a clue to the answer. Listed below are important cue words to look for.

never	not	always	worst	none	every
invariably	less	best	all	often	bad
good	seldom	exactly	fewer	some	more
most	many	usually	equal	sometimes	

29 Follow directions for marking your answers.

Carefully follow directions for marking your answers. Watch for words like *underline*, *write T or F*, *write + or —*, *write True or False*, or *circle the letter of the correct answer*.

30 Mark your answers without looking for a pattern.

Don't try to look for a pattern to the answers. It may seem like every other answer is true or that there are always three false answers in a row, but there's probably no pattern.

31 Write clearly.

Double-check your work to make sure your teacher can read your answers. Write clearly when marking a *T* for true questions and an *F* for false questions so your teacher can tell your letters apart.

32 Answer the easiest questions first.

Skip the hard questions and answer the easiest questions first. Put an **X** beside any question you skipped to remind yourself to come back to the question later.

15 Ways to Answer True/False Questions, *continued*

33 Look at the entire statement.

All parts of the statement must be true for the question to be marked TRUE. If any part of the statement is not true, mark the question FALSE. Here's an example.

_____F_____ 1. Oranges, bananas, and hamburgers are all fruits.

You know that oranges and bananas are fruits. Because a hamburger is not a fruit, this statement is FALSE.

34 Look for exceptions to a statement.

If you can think of one exception to a statement, the answer is FALSE. If you can't think of an exception, mark the answer TRUE.

35 Focus on the question you're answering.

Choose an answer for the question on the test. Don't try to think of other things the statement might mean. Look at this example.

_____T_____ 1. Poems and fairy tales are forms of literature.

You know that poems and fairy tales are forms of literature, but they're not the only forms. What about short stories? What about folktales? You might think this statement is false because it doesn't name all the forms of literature. But don't be fooled! Answer the question as it appears on the test.

36 Look for cue words often used in FALSE questions.

Questions are usually FALSE when they state that something is *always* TRUE. Below is a list of cue words often used in FALSE questions.

never	always	not	none	every
best	worst	exactly	all	invariably
only	first	totally	because	

37 Look for cue words often used in TRUE questions.

Here are some cue words that may tell you a statement is true.

bad	occasionally	less	usually	good
more	generally	seldom	sometimes	many
may	equally	mainly	probably	fewer
most	frequently	often	might	some

15 Ways to Answer True/False Questions, *continued*

38 Identify double negatives in statements.

A double negative is a statement that uses two "negative" words. Here's the strategy for correctly answering statements that contain double negatives.

- Underline both negative words.
- Change the negative words to positive words.
- Reread the statement.
- Choose your answer.

Here's a list of some common negative words.

is not	will not	could not
isn't	won't	couldn't
do not	cannot	should not
don't	can't	shouldn't

39 Identify negative words and negative prefixes in statements.

Negative words and negative prefixes can change the meanings of true/false statements. Negative words are words like *never* and *not*.

Some negative prefixes are *un*, *in*, *im*, *dis*, and *ir*. They mean **not**. For example, if something is **im**possible, it is **not** possible.

40 Guess at questions you're unsure of.

Ask your teacher if there's a penalty for an incorrect answer. You have nothing to lose if there isn't a penalty, so always take a guess at questions you're unsure of.

41 Keep your original answer, unless you're sure it's wrong.

Once you've answered a question, don't change the answer unless you're sure it's wrong. Your first choice is usually correct.

 **Cue Words**

Name _____

Cue words are important words. They help you decide if a statement is true or false.

You'll find important cue words in the word box below. Use it to help you underline the cue words in the following statements. The first one is done for you.

never	always	worst	invariably	many	not
seldom	usually	some	sometimes	most	all

1. Hurricanes <u>usually</u> travel in southern directions.

2. Many masses of circulating air are called *cyclones*.

3. Tornadoes are sometimes called *twisters*.

4. Most tornadoes hit without warning.

5. The worst place to be in a tornado is underground.

6. The midwest section of the country never has tornadoes.

7. Some people ignore weather warnings.

8. Many hurricanes occur in the eastern section of the United States.

9. Hurricanes seldom hit the east coast of Florida.

10. Heavy rains do not accompany hurricanes.

11. A tornado will invariably turn into a hurricane.

12. All tropical storms develop into hurricanes.

13. Some people have lived through many hurricanes.

14. A major hurricane always occurs in June.

15. Hurricanes are the worst natural disaster people experience.

 **Cue Word Clues**

Name _____

The word box shows cue words that say something is *always* TRUE. Statements with these cue words are usually FALSE because few things are true all of the time.

Underline the cue words in the sentences below. Then, circle the word *True* if the statement is true and *False* if the statement is false. The first one is done for you.

all	never	worst	none	only	always	invariably
not	every	best	first	exactly	totally	because

True (False)   1. All animals travel in packs.

True False   2. Male lions never care for their cubs.

True False   3. Insect colonies are the worst organized animal group.

True False   4. None of the animals who live in the ocean migrates in the winter.

True False   5. Lions are the only jungle animals that hunt in groups.

True False   6. Geese always fly in a "V" formation.

True False   7. Monarch butterflies travel exactly 80 miles each day when they migrate to Mexico.

True False   8. The polar regions of the Earth are totally without wildlife.

True False   9. Owls are not able to protect themselves against attackers.

True False   10. Sea lions are always playful.

True False   11. Honeybees are found in every ecosystem on Earth.

True False   12. Gray wolves will invariably travel alone.

True False   13. Gophers are only found on the prairies.

True False   14. Squirrels are the best food source for large animals.

More Cue Word Clues   Name _____

You'll find cue words often used with TRUE statements in the word box below. These cue words are less specific. They say that something **may** be true or is **sometimes** true, rather than is **always** true.

Underline the cue words in the sentences below. Then, circle the word *True* if the statement is true and *False* if the statement is false. The first one is done for you.

many	seldom	generally	probably	frequently	more
usually	often	occasionally	mainly	sometimes	might

(True) False   1. <u>Many</u> years ago people farmed and hunted for their food.

True False   2. Generally, food doesn't grow well when there's been little rainfall.

True False   3. People from different countries probably communicate more now than they did in the past.

True False   4. Advances in technology have been made often in the last 100 years.

True False   5. Teenagers have more in common with each other than they do with adults.

True False   6. People from the same culture usually have many things in common.

True False   7. A culture frequently has distinctive clothing, food, music, and customs.

True False   8. Large ethnic groups are mainly found in or near large cities.

True False   9. Ethnic restaurants are seldom difficult to find in large cities.

True False   10. The language of a group of people can often be linked to the group's culture.

True False   11. Sometimes we add words from other cultures to our language.

True False   12. People occasionally discriminate against members of other cultures.

True False   13. Learning a second language might help you communicate with people from other cultures.

It's an Exception

Name _____

If you can think of one exception to a statement, the question is FALSE. If you can't think of an exception to a statement, the question is TRUE.

Think of one exception to each statement, and write it on the line below the statement. The first one is done for you.

1. All cars have automatic transmissions.

   My sister's car has a stick shift. _____

2. All students graduate from high school when they're 18 years old.

   _____

3. Twins look exactly alike.

   _____

4. Children don't learn to read until they go to school.

   _____

5. Everyone must have a middle name.

   _____

6. You can't play cards unless you have two players.

   _____

7. Trees are bare in the winter.

   _____

8. Squares are the only geometric shape with four sides.

   _____

9. All people in the United States speak English at home.

   _____

10. Every student gets a driver's license at age 16.

    _____

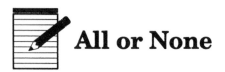 **All or None**

Name _____

All parts of a statement must be true in order for the answer to be TRUE. If any part of a statement is false, the answer is FALSE.

All of the statements below are false. Circle the part of each statement that makes it false. The first one is done for you.

1. Good workers are honest, hard-working, (lazy,) and punctual.

2. Buses, bicycles, and trains are forms of mass transportation.

3. Florida, Minnesota, California, and Texas are states with warm winter climates.

4. You need two teams of seven players, an umpire, equipment, and a field to play baseball.

5. Africa, Australia, and Asia are the three largest continents.

6. Silk, cotton, and cinnamon are kinds of cloth.

7. All mammals are warm-blooded, covered with fur, and produce milk to feed their young.

8. All reptiles are cold-blooded, crawl on their bellies or creep on short legs, and live in the water.

9. Massachusetts, Pennsylvania, Texas, and New York are some of the original colonies of the United States.

10. Citrus fruit, wheat, and corn are the chief crops grown in the midwestern United States.

11. A person must be 18 years old and born in the United States to vote in a national election.

12. White hair, stiff joints, and stronger bones are signs of age.

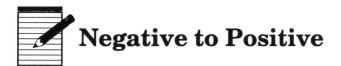

Negative to Positive

Name _____

A double negative is a statement that uses two "negative" words like, "If you *don't* put gas in the car, it *won't* start." Here's a way to figure out whether a statement with a double negative is true or false.

First, underline the negative words in each statement below. Next, rewrite the statement changing the negative words to positive words. Then, circle the word *True* if the statement is true and *False* if the statement is false. The first one is done for you.

(True) False   1. If you don't put gas in the car, it won't start.

If you put gas in the car, it will start. _____

True   False   2. Soup that is not hot will not cool.

_____

True   False   3. If you don't study hard, you will not fail.

_____

True   False   4. You cannot learn to shoot baskets if you do not practice.

_____

True   False   5. A person shouldn't volunteer for a job if she cannot do the work.

_____

True   False   6. If you don't throw gasoline on a burning fire, it will not go out.

_____

True   False   7. A business that does not listen to the needs of its customers will not be successful.

_____

True   False   8. If people don't eat nutritious foods, they won't get sick.

_____

True   False   9. If you don't work, you won't have spending money.

_____

 **Word Play**

Name _____

Negative words and negative prefixes can change the meanings of true/false statements. Negative words are words like *never* and *not*. Some negative prefixes that mean **not** are *un*, *in*, *im*, *dis*, and *ir*.

Underline the cue word in each statement. Then, circle the word *True* if the question is true and the word *False* if the question is false. The first one is done for you.

(True) False   1. The United States was <u>never</u> ruled by a king and a queen.

True False   2. A shark is not a fish.

True False   3. The child climbing the rocks is inactive.

True False   4. A kind person is impolite.

True False   5. Studying hard never helps you improve your grades.

True False   6. Incomplete sentences have a subject and a verb.

True False   7. Birds are unable to fly when they are first hatched.

True False   8. An ear infection is an incurable illness.

True False   9. Irresponsible people make good leaders.

True False   10. Carrots are an unlikely source of vitamins in our diets.

True False   11. Young children are never impatient.

True False   12. An ancient arrowhead is not an artifact.

True False   13. It's improper to thank someone for his help.

True False   14. Students like it when their teachers disapprove of them.

True False   15. Plants never grow in the sunlight.

True False   16. It's impossible to start a campfire without matches.

 **Practice Test**

Name _____

True/False Statements

Circle the word *True* if the statement is true. Circle the word *False* if the statement is false.

True   False   1. South America isn't a continent.

True   False   2. Peninsulas are totally surrounded by water.

True   False   3. People usually consider oxygen the most important gas in the atmosphere for humans.

True   False   4. Deserts are always dry regions of land.

True   False   5. All plants grow on land.

True   False   6. Plant life may be found in the desert.

True   False   7. Rubber is an inflexible material.

True   False   8. The people of a region are seldom affected by its climate.

True   False   9. Cool temperatures are never present near the equator.

True   False   10. Mammals are the only groups of animals to make milk for feeding their young.

True   False   11. Mammals are unable to survive in cold climates.

True   False   12. Irrational thinkers don't always make good decisions.

Practice Test, *continued*

True   False   13. You can't make change for a dollar bill if you don't have four coins.

True   False   14. Six dimes is the same as 60 cents.

True   False   15. Every thermometer shows both Centigrade and Farenheit scales.

True   False   16. If you disagree with a student senate candidate, you probably won't vote for her.

True   False   17. Robert is not an uncommon name.

True   False   18. Oregano, pepper, gravel, and parsley are common spices.

True   False   19. States that don't control what's dumped into their rivers shouldn't expect their drinking water to be clean.

True   False   20. It's uncommon for someone to drink a lot of water after a hard workout.

True   False   21. All of the food we eat is grown in our country.

True   False   22. Babies frequently cry when they're hungry.

True   False   23. Students who do not try their best will not be proud.

True   False   24. New sources of energy might be found in the next 50 years.

True   False   25. Immovable objects are easy to lift.

Unit 3: Multiple Choice Questions

Overview

> Focus . . . . **page 44**
> 1 Handout. . . . . **pages 45-48**
> 7 Activity Sheets . . . . **pages 49-55**
> Practice Test . . . . **pages 56-57**

Multiple choice items are one of the most useful types of objective test questions. This format is also one of the formats most frequently used by educators and can be found on most standardized tests. Like true/false statements, multiple choice items simply ask your students to select the best or the correct answer.

This unit will focus on teaching your students success strategies for becoming more proficient at selecting the best or the correct answer when presented with multiple choice items. Student objectives include:

❏ Understanding general tips for taking multiple choice tests.

❏ Learning to respond to *best answer* or *correct answer* commands.

❏ Knowing the difference between an *item stem* and *item choices*.

❏ Recognizing key words found in multiple choice items.

❏ Recognizing "distractors" in multiple choice items.

You can help your students perform better on multiple choice tests by evaluating your method of writing items. The teacher tips below give you information to consider when writing tests.

Teacher Tips for Test Construction

Arrange answers vertically rather than horizontally, unless they're one-word choices.

Instruct students to circle the letter of the correct answer instead of writing the letter on a blank. This eliminates errors in transferring answers to the blanks.

Use parallel form, such as all nouns or all verb phrases, when constructing answer choices.

Avoid complex choices, such as A & B, B & C, and All of the Above.

Focus

Multiple Choice Questions *(page 44)*

Your students probably don't realize the number of choices they have and the decisions they make every day. After your students have read the focus, discuss choices they've had for different situations. How did they decide which choice was the best one for them? Remind your students that this unit will teach them strategies for selecting the best or correct answers to multiple choice items on tests.

Handout

19 Ways to Answer Multiple Choice Questions *(page 45)*

This handout gives your students detailed strategies for correctly answering multiple choice questions. Use it as a springboard for class discussion to familiarize your students with the language of testing. Encourage them to refer to this handout before and during any test that includes multiple choice questions.

Activity Sheets

What's the Direction? *(page 49)*

Help your students understand the difference between looking for the *correct* answer to a question and looking for the *best* answer to a question. Discuss the importance of carefully reading the directions for each test item or section so your students can decide if they're looking for the *best* answer or the *correct* answer.

Multiple Parts *(page 50)*

This activity gives your students practice identifying the parts of multiple choice items. Tell your students that all multiple choice questions have two parts. The question or statement is called the *stem*, and the possible answers are called *choices*.

Question Type *(page 51)*

Tell your students that the stems of multiple choice questions can be separated into two types. One type is an *incomplete statement* (IS), and the other type is a *question* (Q). The answer your students choose for an incomplete statement will complete the statement. The answer they choose for a question will answer the question. Both types of stems are followed by several choices.

Key Words *(page 52)*

Identifying key words in multiple choice stems helps your students eliminate incorrect choices. Encourage your students to underline key words, such as *not, except, false, incorrect, cannot,* and *only* before attempting to answer a question.

Attempt An Answer *(page 53)*

This strategy teaches your students to answer questions before looking at the choices.

- Read the stem only.
- Try to answer the question without looking at the choices.
- Write your answer in the margin of your paper.
- Look at the choices to see if your answer is a possibility.

Does It Make Sense? *(page 54)*

Tell your students they can decrease the number of choices by eliminating some answers. First, tell them to try each of the choices in the blank to see if it makes sense. Then, they should lightly cross out any choices that don't make sense.

Distractors! *(page 55)*

Distractors are incorrect choices that often have nothing to do with the stems. Encourage your students to look for distractors so they can eliminate them as possible choices. Some cue words that signal distractors are *all, none, never,* and *always*.

Practice Test

Give your students the practice test as a pretest to this unit and as a posttest to assess their progress answering multiple choice questions. Encourage your students to use the handout from this unit to help them with the posttest.

Focus: Multiple Choice Questions

Choices, choices! You make hundreds of choices every day when you decide things like:

- whether to take a shower before or after breakfast

- which jeans to wear to school

- which part-time job to take

- what's the best time to do homework

- which movie to see

All of these things have lots of possibilities. How do you decide which one to choose? Whether you're trying to decide which tennis shoes to buy or which TV program to watch, you need to look closely at all of the possible choices and make the correct or the best selection for you.

Choosing a brand or style of tennis shoes may be more fun than choosing an answer on a test item, but you must also make choices at test time when you're asked to respond to multiple choice items. Multiple choice questions are a popular format with teachers, and you'll probably see them often on tests. The tips in this section will help you narrow down the choices on multiple choice items so you can select the best or the correct answer. You may not learn how to choose the best pair of tennis shoes, but you will learn to be a better test taker!

19 Ways to Answer Multiple Choice Questions

You probably have multiple choice questions on many of the tests you take. Here are 19 tips to help you correctly choose your answers.

42   Identify the two parts of multiple choice questions.

Multiple choice questions have two parts. The question or statement is called the *stem*. The possible answers are called *choices*. Look at this example.

stem   1. _____ is a volcano in Sicily.

choices
- a. Mount Fuji
- b. Mount St. Helens
- c. Mount Etna
- d. Mount Tambora

43   Identify the type of question you're answering.

There are two types of multiple choice stems. One is called an *incomplete statement*. This type of question asks you to provide missing information. You select a choice that *completes* the statement.

A *question* is another type of stem. This type of stem asks you to choose the answer to a question.

44   Decide if you're looking for the *correct* answer or the *best* answer.

Read the directions carefully. When the directions ask you to choose the *correct* answer, only one of the choices is correct. When the directions instruct you to choose the *best* answer, two or more choices may be correct. You need to select the *best* one.

45   Try to answer the question before looking at the choices.

After you read the stem, try to write your answer in the margin of your paper without looking at the choices. Then, look at the choices to see if your answer is a possibility.

46   Read all of the choices before marking your answer.

Make sure you read all of the choices before making your selection. Sometimes there will be more than one correct answer to a question. You want to make sure you're choosing the *best* answer.

19 Ways to Answer Multiple Choice Questions, *continued*

47   **Try each choice in the blank.**

If an answer doesn't come to mind when you read the stem, try each of the possible choices in the blank to see if it makes sense. If a choice doesn't make sense, lightly cross it out. This will help you eliminate some answers.

48   **Answer the questions you know first.**

You'll save time if you answer the questions you know first. Save the questions you don't know until last.

49   **Look carefully for distractors.**

A distractor is an incorrect choice. Many times a distractor doesn't have anything to do with the stem. A distractor may also contain the words *all*, *none*, *never*, or *always*. In the example below, choices **B** and **D** are distractors.

   1.   Which is an ingredient used in oatmeal bars?

   A.   oranges

   B.   never salt

   C.   oatmeal

   D.   use a mixing bowl to stir

50   **Identify cue words often used with incorrect choices.**

If you don't know the correct answer and your selection will be a guess, first look for cue words. Here's a list of cue words normally used with incorrect answers.

never	not	always	none	every
all	exactly	totally	only	

51   **Draw a line through incorrect choices.**

Reduce the number of items you have to choose from by drawing a line through the choices you know are incorrect.

52   **Identify cue words often used with correct choices.**

Below is a list of cue words often used with correct choices.

most	more	less	some
many	usually	generally	probably

19 Ways to Answer Multiple Choice Questions, *continued*

53 **Write a brief rationale for choosing an answer.**

If there are two choices that you think are equally correct, select your best choice. Then, write a brief rationale in the margin of your paper telling why you selected that choice. You may get partial credit for an incorrect answer if you give a good explanation of why you chose that answer.

54 **Use other questions as clues.**

Look for information in the question stems that may be able to help you answer other questions. Look at this example.

1. _____ is a volcano in Sicily.

   A. Mount Fuji

   B. Mount St. Helens

   C. Mount Etna

   D. Mount Tambora

2. Mount Etna is a _____ in Sicily.

   A. restaurant

   B. volcano

   C. famous city

   D. kind of car

You can use the information from the stem in the first question to help you answer the second question.

55 **Follow grammar rules as possible clues to answers.**

"An" is usually used when the answer begins with a vowel (a, e, i, o, u). "A" is usually used when the answer begins with a consonant. For example, **d** is the correct choice for the question below.

1. An _____ is a red fruit.

   a. ketchup

   b. tomato

   c. watermelon

   d. apple

47

56   **Choose "All of the above" if you're unsure of the answer.**

If you're not sure which selection is correct, choose "All of the above" if it's an answer choice.

57   **Read each choice with the stem.**

When a choice indicates that two selections are correct, read each selection carefully with the stem before marking your answer. For example, if one of the choices is A & B, read answer A with the stem. Then, read answer B with the stem. Both must be correct to choose A & B as your answer.

58   **Answer all of the questions.**

Ask your teacher if there's a penalty for an incorrect answer. If there isn't a penalty, always answer every question—even if you have to guess.

59   **Check your work.**

When you've finished the test, go back and check your work to make sure you've responded to each question.

60   **Have faith in yourself.**

As you're checking your work, trust your first instinct. Don't change your answer unless you're sure that your first answer is incorrect.

What's the Direction?

Name _____

Read each set of directions below. Decide if you're asked to find the *best* answer or the *correct* answer. Draw a line under the cue word that tells you what kind of answer you're looking for. The first one is done for you.

1. In the items listed below, circle the correct answer.

2. Underline the best answer for the questions listed below.

3. Fill in the circle of the correct ending to each statement.

4. Write the letter of the correct name on the line next to each question.

5. Circle the best choice for each item.

6. Choose the correct phrase to complete each statement.

7. Write the location of the best place to keep each item.

8. Describe the best way to study for a math test.

9. Place the number of the correct answer in each blank.

10. Circle the correct answer for each question below.

11. Finish each sentence with the best word or phrase.

12. Finish each sentence with the correct word or phrase.

13. Which statement is correct?

14. Which is the best answer?

 **Multiple Parts**   Name _____

All multiple choice questions have two parts. The question or statement is called the *stem*. The possible answers are called *choices*.

Label the stem and the choices for each question below. The first one is done for you.

stem 1. _____ is a volcano in Sicily.
choices ⌐A. Mount Fuji   C. Mount Etna
         └B. Mount St. Helens   D. Mount Tambora

2. The word *innocent* means _____ .
   ⌐A. not guilty
   │ B. slow
   │ C. predict
   └D. large animal

3. Which rock listed below is not an igneous rock?
   ⌐A. basalt   B. gabbro   C. granite   D. limestone

4. The Queen of England is _____ .
   ⌐a. Elizabeth   c. Debra
   └b. Suzanne   d. Isabelle

5. Which food below contains the most salt?
   ⌐a. apples   b. ice cream   c. pickles   d. potatoes

6. If you're outside during a lightning storm, you should _____ .
   ⌐a. stand under a tree
   │ b. get away from tall objects
   │ c. hold onto a metal umbrella
   └d. go inside

Question Type

Name _____

There are two types of multiple choice stems. An *incomplete statement* asks you to provide missing information. A *question* asks you to choose the answer to a question.

Label each stem below as either an incomplete statement (IS) or as a question (Q). You don't need to answer the questions. The first two are done for you.

__IS__   1. There are _____ days in the week.
      A. 6
      B. 5
      C. 7

__Q__   2. How many days are in a week?
      A. 6
      B. 5
      C. 7

_____   3. A type of sedimentary rock is _____ .
      A. granite
      B. marble
      C. sandstone

_____   4. Which rock can be classified as an igneous rock?
      A. basalt
      B. shale
      C. slate

_____   5. Sandstone is a _____ rock.
      A. igneous
      B. sedimentary
      C. none of the above

_____   6. To which class of rocks does marble belong?
      A. igneous
      B. metamorphic
      C. none of the above

 **Key Words**   Name _____

Key words are important words. They help you eliminate incorrect choices. That's why it's important to identify key words in stems before you try to answer questions.

You'll find key words in the word box. Use it to help you underline the key word in each stem below. You don't need to answer the questions. The first one is done for you.

not	except	false	incorrect	cannot	only

1. Which rock <u>cannot</u> be classified as an igneous rock?

2. All of the rocks listed below are igneous rocks except _____ .

3. Which rock is incorrectly listed as a sedimentary rock?

4. Which rock is not a sedimentary rock?

5. The only rock that is not igneous is _____ .

6. All of the stones listed below are gems except _____ .

7. Which statement about silver is false?

8. Draw a line through the incorrect items listed below as precious metals.

9. Which metal should not be used to make drinking cups?

10. Which mineral cannot be placed in this group?

11. The human body needs all of the following minerals except _____ .

12. Underline the false statement about minerals in our diets.

Attempt An Answer

Name _____

Have you ever tried to think of the answer to a multiple choice question before looking at the choices? If you haven't, try this strategy. If the answer you think of on your own is one of the choices, it's probably the correct choice.

- Read the stem only.
- Try to answer the question without looking at the choices.
- Write your answer in the margin of your paper.
- Look at the choices to see if your answer is a possibility.

Read each question below. Try to answer the questions before looking at the choices.

1. How many months are in a year?
   a. 10   b. 8   c. 12   d. 11

2. How many days are in a week?
   a. 7   b. 8   c. 6   d. 9

3. How many days are in a year?
   a. 360   b. 365   c. 460   d. 367

4. How many weeks are in a year?
   a. 30   b. 25   c. 52   d. 50

5. How many days are in the longest month of the year?
   a. 30   b. 31   c. 40   d. 35

6. How many days are in the shortest month of the year?
   a. 28   b. 15   c. 25   d. 31

7. How many years are in a decade?
   a. 1   b. 10   c. 13   d. 100

8. Which month is near the end of the year?
   a. April   b. February   c. May   d. November

Does It Make Sense?

Name _____

Sometimes you won't be able to think of an answer without looking at the choices. When this happens, try each of the choices in the blank of an incomplete sentence to see if it makes sense.

Use this tip as you circle the letter of the correct choice for each question below.

1. Leap year adds _____ more day(s) to the year.

    a. one   b. two   c. three   d. four

2. There are _____ years in a decade.

    a. ten   b. one   c. twenty   d. one hundred

3. There are _____ decades in a century.

    a. 50   b. 5   c. 10   d. 4

4. There are _____ years in a century.

    a. 100   b. 50   c. 365   d. 99

5. An _____ is the yearly celebration of an event.

    a. octave   b. opening   c. anniversary   d. ending

6. Flowers that come up every year without replanting are called _____ .

    a. bouquets   b. seedlings   c. weaklings   d. perennials

7. The one hundred year anniversary of an event is called the _____ .

    a. marathon   b. centennial   c. biannual   d. silver anniversary

8. The Winter Olympics are held every _____ years.

    a. four   b. ten   c. twenty   d. one hundred

Distractors!

Name _____

A distractor is an incorrect choice. Many times a distractor doesn't have anything to do with the stem. A distractor may also contain the words *all*, *none*, *never*, or *always*.

Underline the distractors in each question below. Then, circle the letter of the correct choice.

1. How many Presidents serve the United States at one time?

    A. five

    B. always two

    C. one

    D. all of the above

2. How many votes does each United States citizen have when voting for the President?

    A. one

    B. two

    C. three

    D. all of the above

3. The President's wife is called _____ .

    A. Mrs. President

    B. the Vice President

    C. never the First Lady

    D. the First Lady

4. Who was the first President of the United States?

    A. Bill Clinton

    B. George Washington

    C. John F. Kennedy

    D. None of the above

5. Which President lived in a log cabin?

    A. Bill Clinton

    B. Abraham Lincoln

    C. John F. Kennedy

    D. None of the above

 **Practice Test**

Multiple Choice

Circle the letter of the correct choice for each item below.

1. In most parts of the country, which season would be too cold for flowers to bloom?

   A. fall

   B. winter

   C. always spring

   D. summer

2. Which of the following helps grass grow?

   A. planting trees

   B. always building protective barriers

   C. watering infrequently

   D. watering frequently

3. Which is the best answer?

   A. Plant flowers in the fall.

   B. Plant flowers in the winter.

   C. Plant flowers in the spring.

   D. Plant flowers in the summer.

4. Which statement is correct?

   A. Erosion (wearing away of soil) is caused by water.

   B. Erosion is caused by wind.

   C. Erosion is caused by ice.

   D. All of the above.

5. A large, slow-moving mass of ice is called a _____ .

   A. glacier

   B. delta

   C. always a lake

   D. all of the above

6. Top soil is _____ .

   A. never on top

   B. called a delta

   C. the richest part of soil

   D. none of the above

7. The coldest season of the year is called _____ .

   A. fall

   B. winter

   C. spring

   D. summer

8. Another word for spine is _____ .

   A. always a knee

   B. nose

   C. backbone

   D. always the skull

9. A spy is someone who _____ .

   A. does secret work

   B. is a movie star

   C. never works for the police

   D. all of the above

10. Which of the following would you find in a band?

    A. dynamite

    B. always a fire hydrant

    C. cymbals

    D. a gym

57

Unit 4: Matching Questions

Overview

Like true/false statements and multiple choice items, matching test questions measure factual information and are based on simple associations. They measure a student's proficiency in simple recognition of items.

Matching items are popular with teachers because the format is an efficient method of measuring simple relationships. The matching format is used more frequently by educators for measuring retention of information and is not often found on standardized tests.

In this unit, your students will learn and practice the following strategies for becoming more proficient at answering matching questions.

- ❏ Understanding general responses for test-taking tips to use with matching test formats.

- ❏ Learning to focus more efficiently on test directions.

- ❏ Developing strategies for responding to matching formats.

- ❏ Understanding ways to reduce memory load when responding to lengthy matching formats.

You can help your students perform better on matching tests by evaluating your method of writing items. The teacher tips below give you information to consider when writing tests.

Teacher Tips for Test Construction

Avoid long matching lists.

Keep items brief.

Provide only one correct answer for each item.

Place longer items on the left. Place blanks for answers in between the two columns rather than in the margin.

Avoid having students match items by drawing lines. This becomes confusing, especially if a student needs to erase.

Provide an extra response in one of the columns. If a student mismatches an item, the chance of mismatching another one is decreased.

Focus

Matching Questions *(page 61)*

Before introducing the focus, talk about different matching exercises your students go through each day. The focus explains how these everyday matching exercises are similar to tests they take at school.

Handout

10 Ways to Answer Matching Questions *(page 62)*

The format of matching tests can be confusing for your students, especially when more than one choice is correct or there are an equal number of choices. This handout gives your students detailed strategies for responding to matching items on tests. Encourage them to refer to this handout before and during any test that includes matching questions.

Activity Sheets

Is It Clear? *(page 64)*

Your students can lose valuable points if they don't follow the test directions correctly. This activity gives your students practice following directions on matching items.

How Many Choices? *(page 65)*

Ask your students what might happen if they chose the first flavor listed at a frozen yogurt stand without reading all of the possible choices. Tell your students they should read all of the items in both columns on a matching test for the same reasons, especially when they're looking for the best answer.

Starting Point *(page 66)*

This strategy gives your students a sequence of steps to follow when answering matching questions. The focus is on the starting point.

- Start with the first item in the first column.
- Scan the other column to find the correct answer.
- Skip the item and go to the second item if you don't see the answer.

Speech Parts *(page 67)*

Review what nouns and verbs are with your students. When matching synonyms or other word-for-word items, parts of speech can be clues to a correct choice if your students are unsure of the answer. Remind them that a noun will match a noun, and a verb will match a verb.

Matching Mania *(page 68)*

This activity gives your students practice matching a phrase or a sentence with a one- or two-word choice. The strategy here is to begin working from the column with the longest choices and match them with the one- or two-word choices in the other column.

Practice Test

Give your students the practice test as a pretest to this unit and as a posttest to assess their progress answering matching questions. Encourage your students to use the handout from this unit to help them with the posttest.

Focus: Matching Questions

- Are you confused when taking a matching test because you can't decide which answer goes with which statement?

- Do you get discouraged when several choices seem to match an item on a matching test?

- Have you lost points on a matching test because time ran out and you still had items left to match to correct answers?

- Would you like to improve your matching test scores?

If you answered YES to any of these questions, then read on! You may not realize it, but you make matching choices every day. Each morning when you're getting ready for school, you actually go through a matching exercise. Which shirt matches your jeans or skirt? Which pair of socks looks best? You're put to the test—a matching test.

The tests you take at school are like the matching exercise you do with your clothes each morning. You must decide which choice goes best with an item. This unit will help you improve your test-taking skills by teaching you tips that will help you with matching tests. So get ready to be a better "match maker" at test time!

10 Ways to Answer Matching Questions

Matching questions can be confusing, especially if more than one choice sounds correct. These ten tips will help you choose your answers.

61 **Ask if there's a penalty for incorrect answers.**

Unless there's a penalty for incorrect answers, complete all of the questions—even if you have to guess some answers.

62 **Read the directions carefully.**

Make sure you're doing what the directions ask you to do, like *match items* or *put the correct number next to the word it matches*. You don't want to lose points because you marked your answers incorrectly.

63 **Read all the items in both columns before you begin to answer.**

Sometimes more than one answer will match an item. When this happens, it's easy to get mixed-up. You need to read all the items in both columns so you have more information to use when answering the question. That way you'll be able to select the *best* choice.

64 **Match the items you know first.**

First answer the items you know are correct. Then, use the remaining choices to go back and answer the items that are left.

65 **Start with the first item in the first column.**

The first column is the one the direction mentions first. For example, **Column B** is the first column in the direction below.

Match the definitions in Column B to words in Column A.

To follow this direction, you should look at the first definition in Column B. Then, scan Column A to find the correct word. If you don't see it, go to the second definition in Column B. You can come back to the first definition later.

66 **Draw a line through answers you've used.**

After you choose an answer, lightly mark through it with your pencil. This will help you keep track of the choices you've used.

10 Ways to Answer Matching Questions, *continued*

67   **Begin with the column with the longest choices.**

Sometimes you'll be asked to match a phrase or sentence with a one- or two-word choice. When this happens, start at the column with the longest choices—the one with the most reading. Match these items with the shorter choices.

68   **Narrow down the choices.**

If you think that two or three answers may be possible for an item, write the letters or numbers of possible choices next to it. This will help you narrow down the choices.

69   **See how many choices are in each column.**

Some matching tests will have an equal number of choices in each column. Other matching tests will have extra choices that won't be used. Before you begin to answer, check to see if the number of choices in each column is the same. If it isn't the same, you'll know there will be choices you won't use.

70   **Check the part of speech when matching synonyms.**

When you're matching synonyms, always check the part of speech. A noun will match a noun and a verb will match a verb.

 **Is It Clear?**

Name _____

It's important to understand the test directions so you mark your answers correctly. Study the list of directions below and complete the exercises. The first one is done for you

1. Match the statements in Column B with the correct responses in Column A.

Column A	Column B
___C___ Mouth	A. the process of changing food into substances the body can use
_____ Digestion	B. moves food around in the mouth
_____ Tongue	C̸. where digestion begins
_____ Teeth	D. breaks up food into small pieces
	E. secretes juices into the mouth

2. Match the following items.

Mouth _____	A. the process of changing food into substances the body can use
Digestion _____	B. moves food around in the mouth
Tongue _____	C. where digestion begins
Teeth _____	D. breaks up food into small pieces
	E. secretes juices into the mouth

3. Place the correct number in the blank provided.

_____ Mouth	1. the process of changing food into substances the body can use
_____ Digestion	2. moves food around in the mouth
_____ Tongue	3. where digestion begins
_____ Teeth	4. breaks up food into small pieces
	5. secretes juices into the mouth

How Many Choices?

Name _____

Sometimes more than one choice will match an item. To make sure you're selecting the best answer, first read all the items in both columns so you know which choices are possible. Then, begin matching items.

Match the items in Column B that go with the holidays in Column A.

Column A

_____ 1. July 4th

_____ 2. New Year's Eve

_____ 3. Valentine's Day

Column B

A. fireworks

B. candy hearts

C. American flags

Match the foods in Column B that go with the foods in Column A.

Column A

_____ 4. hot dogs

_____ 5. cheese

_____ 6. bacon

_____ 7. steak

_____ 8. peanut butter

_____ 9. mashed potatoes

Column B

A. peaches

B. eggs

C. mustard

D. crackers

E. jelly

F. gravy

G. onions

Match the full titles in Column B with the abbreviations in Column A.

Column A

10. NBA _____

11. NFL _____

12. ABC _____

13. BSA _____

14. TLC _____

15. TGIF _____

Column B

A. American Broadcasting System

B. Boy Scouts of America

C. Tender Loving Care

D. National Basketball Association

E. National Football League

F. National Association of Coaches

G. Thank Goodness It's Friday

Starting Point

Name _____

The first column is the column the directions mention first. Start with the first item in the first column. Then, scan the other column to find the correct answer. If you don't find the answer, skip the item and go on to the next one. You can come back to it later.

Practice this tip as you match the items below.

Match the definitions in Column A to the words in Column B.

Column A	Column B
_____ 1. something that needs to be mowed	A. tracks
_____ 2. something you wear on your wrist	B. grass
_____ 3. a train runs on these	C. fish
_____ 4. used to work in the yard	D. watch
_____ 5. connects two pieces of land	E. rake
_____ 6. found in water	F. bread
	G. bridge

Match the statements in Column A with the correct answers in Column B.

Column A	Column B
_____ 7. In class each person sits in a _____ .	a. nests
_____ 8. A _____ can give you a nasty sting.	b. glass
_____ 9. Birds build _____ .	c. squirrel
_____ 10. We use a _____ to drink water from a glass.	d. desk
_____ 11. A _____ will break if you drop it.	e. straw
_____ 12. A _____ likes to eat nuts.	f. wasp
	g. house

Speech Parts

Name _____

When you're matching synonyms or other word-for-word items, always check the part of speech. A noun will match a noun and a verb will match a verb.

Match the synonyms below. The first item is done for you.

Column A	Column B
__B__ 1. shout (verb)	A. servant (noun)
__A__ 2. maid (noun)	B. yell (verb)
__C__ 3. stroll (verb)	C. walk (verb)

Column A	Column B
_____ 4. hurricane (noun)	A. disappear (verb)
_____ 5. vanish (verb)	B. storm (noun)
_____ 6. father (noun)	C. dad (noun)

Column A	Column B
_____ 7. collide	A. walk
_____ 8. lumber	B. crash
_____ 9. stroll	C. wood

Column A	Column B
_____ 10. machine	A. land
_____ 11. territory	B. engine
_____ 12. gaze	C. stare

Column A	Column B
_____ 13. inquire	A. king
_____ 14. monarch	B. fall
_____ 15. autumn	C. ask

 **Matching Mania**   Name _____

Sometimes the directions will tell you to match a phrase or sentence with a one- or two-word choice. When this happens, start at the column with the longest choices—the one with the most reading. Match these items with the shorter choices.

Use this tip to match the items in the columns below.

1. Match the definitions in Column B with the words in Column A.

Column A	Column B
_____ summer	A. a heavenly body found in the solar system
_____ winter	B. season when the sun is highest
_____ sun	C. season when the sun is lowest
_____ star	D. a shining body visible in the sky at night

2. Match the descriptions in Column A with the words in Column B.

Column A	Column B
_____ a curved metal object used to fasten papers together	a. atlas
_____ a tool with a blunt end used to drive nails into wood	b. hammer
_____ a bowl-shaped object with holes in it used to drain vegetables	c. colander
_____ a grooming aid with a sharp edge used to remove hair from the face	d. pliers
_____ interlocking metal objects that allow a door to swing open or shut	e. razor
_____ a collection of maps bound together in a book	f. hinges
	g. paper clip

 **Practice Test**

Name _____

Matching

Match the definitions in Column B to the correct words in Column A.

Column A

_____ 1. flag

_____ 2. balloon

_____ 3. motion

_____ 4. collide

_____ 5. planets

_____ 6. sunspots

Column B

A. flies in the air

B. heavenly bodies that form the solar system

C. has 50 stars

D. solar activity which may interfere with radio reception on Earth

E. a type of horn

F. crash

G. movement

Match the groups in Column A to their leaders in Column B.

Column A

7. baseball team _____

8. U.S. citizens _____

9. students _____

10. soldiers _____

11. bees _____

12. orchestra _____

Column B

A. general

B. queen

C. operator

D. captain

E. conductor

F. President

G. principal

Unit 5: Completion Questions

Overview

Definition items and open-ended questions can be difficult for many students. A more meaningful way to tap word knowledge may be to ask your students completion questions.

This unit will give your students practice answering completion items with and without word banks. You should consider providing word banks on tests to help students who have difficulty with recall. They also make grading easier by eliminating questions that come up when a student completes a statement logically but doesn't use the word or term you're looking for.

You may decide to give your students a word bank to use when studying rather than providing one on the test. This will help them become familiar with the groups of words and will make it easier for them to recall words at test time.

In this unit, your students learn and practice the following strategies to become more proficient at answering completion questions.

❑ Eliminating incorrect choices.

❑ Using context clues to help choose the correct answer.

❑ Gaining experience and proficiency using a word bank.

❑ Using organizational strategies when working on completion items.

You can help your students perform better on completion questions by evaluating your method of writing and grading items. The teacher tips below give you information to consider when writing and grading tests.

Teacher Tips for Test Construction

Use a key word or term from the sentence as the blank.

Avoid awkward phrasing. Construct sentences that sound logical.

Include context clues in sentences to help students narrow down their answer choices.

When using similar terms or words for answers, provide grammatical cues (a/an, singular/plural) before the blanks to help students distinguish one answer from another.

Include an extra word choice in the word bank when providing one.

Consider answers for partial credit if they reflect general knowledge rather than the specific answer you had in mind.

Focus

Completion Questions *(page 74)*

Before introducing the focus, explain to your students how they use words and terms in context every day when speaking and writing. The focus helps your students understand the importance of using context clues and common sense to answer completion items.

Handout

12 Ways to Answer Completion Questions *(page 75)*

This handout gives your students detailed strategies for answering completion questions. Use it as a springboard for class discussion to familiarize your students with the language of testing. Encourage them to refer to this handout before and during any test that includes completion items.

Activity Sheets

Which Do You Know? *(page 77)*

Tell your students they'll save time if they answer the questions they know first and save the items they don't know until last. They'll also have a better idea of the amount of time they can spend on each item they don't know if they save these until last. This activity gives your students practice with this strategy.

Answer Clues *(page 78)*

Identifying "a" and "an" in completion items can give your students a clue to the answer. Encourage them to look at the word right before the blank. Explain that "a" is usually used when the answer begins with a consonant, and "an" is usually used when the answer begins with a vowel.

Grammar Clues *(page 79)*

Review noun/verb agreement with your students, and explain how it can help them complete items. This activity gives your students practice looking for noun/verb agreement when answering completion items.

Long or Short? *(page 80)*

Your students use the lengths of the blanks as possible clues to answer completion items in this activity. Remind your students that line lengths are only clues some of the time. Sometimes the lengths of the blanks won't mean anything.

Count 'Em! *(page 81)*

Tell your students that the number of blanks in a completion item can also be a clue to the answer. Explain that one blank usually indicates a one-word answer. Two or more blanks usually means the answer is two or more words long. Your students practice completing items with one-, two-, and three-word blanks in this activity.

On Your Own *(page 82)*

This strategy teaches your students how to answer questions when there's a word bank.

- Read the question.
- Try to answer the question without looking at the word bank.
- Check the word bank to see if your answer is a possibility.
- If your answer isn't a possibility, choose a word from the word bank that makes the most sense.
- Cross your answer off the word bank and write it on the blank.

Unused Words *(page 83)*

When a word bank has been provided, what do your students do after they've answered the items they know? This activity teaches your students to use common sense and the process of elimination to complete the unanswered items with the remaining words from the word bank.

Part and Whole *(page 84)*

Sometimes your students will be asked to complete items in a paragraph format rather than in single sentences. Tell them not to panic when presented with this format. This activity teaches your students to complete the blanks in the sentences separately and then go back and read the entire paragraph to see if it makes sense.

Practice Test

Give your students the practice test as a pretest to this unit and as a posttest to assess their progress answering completion questions. Encourage your students to use the handout from this unit to help them with the posttest.

Focus: Completion Questions

Completion items are just another way of asking you a question. For example, instead of asking the open-ended question, "What is your favorite color?" your teacher could say, "My favorite color is _____," and ask you to fill in the blank.

If you have trouble answering completion items, you may not be looking for the clues that help you think of the answer. In fact, completion questions can be easier to answer than open-ended questions because the sentence often gives you a clue to what the answer is. In the example above, the sentence gives you a clue that a color word goes in the blank and not a kind of food, an animal name, or an action word.

This unit will show you how to look for sentence clues to help you answer completion questions. You'll also practice using your common sense to decide if a completion item makes sense with different word choices. This will help you eliminate some incorrect answer choices. When you've finished this unit, you'll have a complete understanding of completion questions!

12 Ways to Answer Completion Questions

There are several clues you can follow to help you answer completion questions. These 12 tips will show you how!

71   **Ask if a word bank will be provided on the test.**

Some completion tests have a word bank and some don't. Ask your teacher if there will be a word bank on your test that you can also use to study.

72   **Look at the length of the blank.**

Sometimes, but not always, the length of the blank will be a clue to the answer. A long blank may be a clue that the answer is a long word. A short blank may be a clue that the answer is a short word.

73   **Look at the number of blanks.**

An answer is usually one word when there's one blank. Two or more blanks usually means the answer is two or more words long.

74   **Try to complete the answer without looking at the word bank.**

If there's a word bank on the test, try to answer the questions without looking at it. If you don't know an answer, then look at the word bank and choose the word that makes the most sense.

75   **Cross off choices in the word bank as you use them.**

If there's a word bank on the test, lightly cross off choices as you use them. This will help you narrow down the number of possible answers you have to choose from for other questions.

76   **Answer remaining items with unused words from the word bank.**

After you've answered all the items you know using the word bank, reread the questions you haven't answered. Use the leftover words in the word bank to fill in the remaining blanks. Choose words that sound correct and make sense.

77   **Answer each sentence separately when completing a paragraph.**

Sometimes you'll be asked to complete words in a paragraph rather than in single sentences. When this happens, first fill in the blanks for each sentence separately. Then, go back and read the whole paragraph to see if it makes sense.

12 Ways to Answer Completion Questions, *continued*

78   **Check to see if the answer is grammatically correct.**

If the sentence is missing a verb, make sure your answer is a verb. If the sentence is missing a noun, make sure your answer is a noun. If you're not sure you've used proper grammar, read the sentence with your answer to see if it makes sense.

79   **Check the word right before the blank.**

"An" is usually used when the answer begins with a vowel (a, e, i, o, u). "A" is usually used when the answer begins with a consonant.

80   **Save the questions you don't know until last.**

Complete the items you know first. Then, come back to the items you don't know and try to complete them.

81   **Answer all of the questions.**

Ask your teacher if there's a penalty for incorrect answers. If there isn't a penalty, complete all of the questions—even if you're unsure of the answer.

82   **Guess if you have to—you may get partial credit.**

If you have to guess an answer, try to guess as close to the correct answer as possible. Sometimes your teacher will give you partial credit for an answer that's close to the correct answer.

 **Which Do You Know?**   Name _____

You'll save time if you complete the answers you know first. Save the items you don't know until last.

Use this tip as you complete the sentences below. The first one is done for you.

1. An _____*eagle*_____ is the bird that symbolizes America.

2. Yellow _____ are used as the symbol of coming home.

3. A _____ cross is the worldwide symbol for first aid.

4. A skull and crossbones on a bottle is the symbol for _____ .

5. SOS is a signal for _____ .

6. A _____ flying at half-mast means that someone has died.

7. Tin cans tied to a car bumper mean that two people have gotten _____ .

8. Yellow tape with a warning on it is put across the door of a building where a _____ has been committed.

9. Blue booties hanging on a mother's door means that a baby _____ has been born.

10. An outline of children on a traffic sign means that a _____ is nearby.

11. Balloons tied to a mailbox might mean that it's someone's _____ .

12. If someone is unable to talk and grasps her throat with her hands, this is a signal that she's _____ .

 **Answer Clues**

Name _____

Check the word right before the blank when answering completion items. "An" is usually used when the answer begins with a vowel (a, e, i, o, u). "A" is usually used when the answer begins with a consonant.

Look at the word before each blank when completing the sentences below. The first one is done for you.

1. A drum is an _*instrument*_ used to keep time.

2. Autumn is a _____ of the year.

3. An _____ is a large sea animal with eight legs.

4. It's useful to carry an _____ when it's raining.

5. If it rains while the sun is shining, a _____ comes out.

6. An insect that helps spread a flower's pollen is a _____ .

7. A piece of jewelry worn on the ear is an _____ .

8. The list of food served at a restaurant is the _____ .

9. A moving stairway is an _____ .

10. An _____ is the name for your aunt's husband.

11. Cloth makes a good _____ to support a broken arm.

12. Coconuts grow on _____ trees.

 **Grammar Clues**

Name _____

If the missing word is the subject of the sentence, check the verb. If the missing word is the verb of the sentence, check the subject.

Make sure there's noun/verb agreement as you complete the sentences below. The first one is done for you.

1. ___*Children*___ play more often than adults.

2. An _____ works more often than a child.

3. _____ build nests to lay their eggs in.

4. An _____ lays bigger eggs than any other bird.

5. A roof _____ a house or a building.

6. When it rains, roofs with holes in them _____ .

7. A speedometer _____ miles traveled per hour.

8. Odometers _____ distance traveled by a vehicle.

9. _____ revolve around the sun. Together they make the solar system.

10. Mercury _____ closest to the sun.

11. A geologist _____ rocks and fossils.

12. Psychologists _____ human behavior.

 **Long or Short?**   Name _____

Sometimes, but not always, the length of the blank will be a clue to the answer. A long blank may be a clue that the answer is a long word. A short blank may be a clue that the answer is a short word.

Use the length of the blank as a clue to answer the questions below about transportation. The first one is done for you.

1. Another name for an automobile is a ___*car*___ .

2. A common name for a boat on the ocean is a _____ .

3. The fastest way to travel from New York to California is by _____ .

4. A _____ is a two-wheeled motorized vehicle.

5. _____ are two-wheeled vehicles that are powered by pedaling.

6. Both schools and cities use _____ to carry many people at one time.

7. Before airplanes were invented, the quickest way to travel across the country was by _____ .

8. In the 1800's, the main form of transportation was by horse and _____ .

9. A _____ is different from an airplane because its propeller is on the top.

10. A _____ is a boat that travels under the water.

11. It's hard to move a _____ across the water when there's no wind.

12. An electrical train that travels underground is called a _____ .

 **Count 'Em!**

Name _____

The number of blanks in a sentence can be a clue to the answer. An answer is usually one word when there's one blank. Two or more blanks usually mean the answer is two or more words long.

Complete each sentence about comics and cartoons with the missing word or words. The first one is done for you.

1. Blondie is married to ___*Dagwood*___ .

2. Lucy never lets _____ _____ kick the football.

3. _____ is a friendly ghost.

4. _____ _____ likes Minnie Mouse.

5. _____ protects Gotham City.

6. _____ _____ _____ is a little boy who bothers Mr. Wilson.

7. _____ _____ lives next to Fred Flintstone.

8. _____ _____ always gets the best of Elmer Fudd.

9. _____ is the cat who loves to eat lasagna and play tricks on Odie.

10. _____ eats spinach to stay strong.

11. Watch out for the _____ _____ if you hear, "beep-beep."

12. _____ _____ lived with the seven dwarfs.

 **On Your Own**

Name _____

If there's a word bank on the test, try to answer the questions without looking at it. If you don't know an answer, then look at the word bank and choose the word that makes the most sense. Cross off each word in the word bank as you use it.

Complete each sentence about your body using the word bank, if necessary. You won't use all of the words. The first one is done for you.

muscles	heart	nerves	liver
esophagus	blood	~~saliva~~	teeth
tonsils	gall bladder	immune system	

1. ____*Saliva*____ often begins the breakdown of starches.

2. Biceps, triceps, and deltoids are all _____ .

3. The _____ pumps blood to all parts of your body.

4. Digestive juice called bile is produced by the _____ .

5. _____ connect parts of the nervous system with other organs.

6. _____ carries oxygen and nourishment to all parts of the body.

7. The _____ _____ stores bile until it's needed for digestion.

8. Your body's _____ _____ helps it fight against disease.

9. _____ are important for breaking down food into smaller pieces.

10. The _____ don't play a part in digestion.

Unused Words

Name _____

First, answer all the items you know and cross off the words you've used from the word bank. Then, reread the questions you haven't answered. Use the leftover words in the word bank to fill in the remaining blanks. Choose words that sound correct and make sense.

twice	~~illness~~	fat	cigarettes
six	walking	stretch	seat belts
milk	physical	healthy	antibiotics

1. A temperature of 104 degrees is a sign of _____*illness*_____ .

2. You should try to drink _____ glasses of water each day.

3. Regular exercise helps keep you _____ .

4. Healthy diets are low in _____ .

5. Wearing _____ _____ saves lives.

6. You should visit the dentist _____ a year.

7. _____ is a good form of exercise.

8. It's a good idea to get an annual _____ from your doctor.

9. Smoking _____ increases your risk of heart and lung disease.

10. You should always _____ before performing any kind of exercise.

11. Drinking _____ helps build strong bones and teeth.

12. _____ help fight infection in your body.

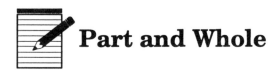

Part and Whole

Name _____

Sometimes you'll be asked to complete words in a paragraph rather than in single sentences. When this happens, first read the entire paragraph. Next, fill in the blanks for each sentence separately. Then, go back and read the whole paragraph to see if it makes sense.

Follow this tip to complete the paragraphs below.

mouth	stomach	salivary glands
tongue	teeth	digestion

1. Food is fuel for the body. When food is broken down into substances the body can

   use, the process is called _____ . Digestion begins in the _____

   where the _____ moves around and the _____ break the food into

   small pieces. While food is in the mouth, the _____ _____

   begin changing starches into sugar.

cigarettes	vegetables	cancer	diet
environment	loud noise	pollution	salt

2. Over the past 25 years, we've learned a lot about good health. We've learned that

   smoking _____ can cause _____ and heart attacks. We know

   that a good _____ includes lots of fruits and _____ . We know

   that things in the _____ can harm us. _____ _____

   can cause us to lose our hearing and _____ can harm our lungs. You have

   to be aware to stay healthy!

 **Practice Test**

Name _____

Completion Questions

Complete the sentences below.

microscope	hypothesis	scientific method	data
classifying	microphone	five senses	

1. Direct observation is made by the _____ _____: touch, sight, hearing, smell, and taste

2. A scientific instrument used to make an indirect observation is a _____.

3. A possible answer or solution to a question is a _____ .

4. Information that is collected and analyzed is called _____.

5. Sorting information into categories is called _____ .

6. The _____ _____ is one way scientists solve problems.

exam	passport	illegal alien	alien
citizen	immigrant	council	

7. A _____ is a member of a society or nation.

8. A person who lives in a country but isn't a citizen is an _____ .

9. An _____ is a person who comes to a new country to live there permanently.

10. A _____ is a document that permits a citizen to travel out of his country.

11. A person who comes into a country without a passport is called an _____ _____ .

12. People who want to become American citizens must pass an _____ .

Unit 6: Definition Questions

Overview

Defining words and using words in context is an expectation of teachers across all content areas. Some teachers use definition tests for weekly spelling vocabulary assessment. Other educators require students to respond to definition items in social studies, literature, or science.

Although popular with teachers, this type of test format can be difficult for many students because it requires structured study and memorizing. The format itself is very flexible; however, it can vary from requiring simple recognition responses to structured recall formats. Matching, true/false, multiple choice, sentence completion with or without word banks, and sentence dictation are the most popular formats for definition tests.

This unit will help your students gain success responding to the numerous tests that require them to "define" words in various testing formats. Your students will be given specific strategies for *studying* for definition tests, as well as a number of detailed tips for *responding* to definition items. Student objectives include:

❏ Learning effective ways of studying for definition tests.

❏ Observing the test blank size as a clue to the correct word choice.

❏ Looking for "a" and "an" and subject/verb agreement as test cues.

❏ Understanding different types of contextual clues for responding to definition items.

You can help your students perform better on definition questions by evaluating your method of writing items. The teacher tips below give you information to consider when writing tests.

Teacher Tips for Test Construction

Let your students know prior to the test if it *will* or *will not* have a word bank.

Select the most important words to be learned. Long lists may result in students learning only a few of the words because too much information was presented.

Select words that have meaning to the students and that relate to the subject matter to be learned and retained.

Present words in context or with cues whenever possible, instead of presenting students with isolated words and asking for a definition.

Focus

Definition Questions *(page 89)*

How well can your students define words? Before introducing the focus, talk to your students about the real-life application of understanding definitions and why educators across all content areas expect their students to define words and use words in context. Explain that definition items may appear in various test formats, but they all require extensive studying and memorizing by your students. This unit will help them study for and respond to definition questions.

Handouts

21 Ways to Answer Definition Questions *(page 90)*

The key to success on definition tests is studying and memorizing. This handout gives your students detailed study techniques for learning definitions and strategies for correctly answering definition questions. Use it as a springboard for class discussion to familiarize your students with the language of testing. Encourage them to refer to this handout before and during any test that includes definition questions.

Prefix and Suffix Meanings *(page 94)*

Learning the meanings of common prefixes and suffixes can give your students an advantage when taking tests that include definition items. Even if the root word is unfamiliar to them, knowing the prefix or suffix gives your students information to use as they make an educated guess at the meaning of a word. This handout lists some common prefixes and suffixes and gives their meanings.

Context Clues *(page 95)*

This handout explains and gives examples of the five kinds of context clues your students can look for to help them with definition items. Before discussing the handout, give each student a copy. Then, have them refer to it as they complete **What's the Context?** on page 99.

87

Activity Sheets

Visual Clues *(page 96)*

This activity gives your students practice answering definition items by providing the missing words in incomplete statements. They're encouraged to look at the number and length of the blanks as possible clues to the answers.

Word Clues *(page 97)*

Some definition items ask your students to fill in the correct word within context. When this happens, looking for "a" and "an" right before the blank in an incomplete statement can give them a clue to the answer. Although not presented in this activity, tell your students that some words that begin with the letter *u*, such as *unicorn*, won't follow this rule.

Subject or Verb? *(page 98)*

Before beginning this activity, review noun/verb agreement with your students. Tell them they can use this rule as a clue when completing definitions within incomplete statements.

What's the Context? *(page 99)*

Give your students the **Context Clues** handout on page 95. Discuss the five types of context clues before beginning this activity. For more of a challenge, when they've finished the activity, ask them to tell you what kind of context clue they used to answer each definition item.

Practice Test

Give your students the practice test as a pretest to this unit and as a posttest to assess their progress answering definition questions. Encourage your students to use the handouts from this unit to help them with the posttest.

Focus: Definition Questions

Why do you need to know what words mean? Knowing the definition of words in movie titles helps you choose the movie that's best for you. Understanding words on a menu helps you choose your favorite foods. Knowing the definitions of words allows you to understand the conversations you have with your friends.

Because knowing what words mean is an important part of everyday life, you'll probably see a lot of definition questions on tests. You may be asked to define a word, complete a sentence with the correct word, or match words to the correct definition. Whatever the test format, being able to answer definition questions is an important skill.

In this unit, you'll learn that studying and memorizing are crucial to your success on definition questions. This unit will teach you a plan for studying and remembering definition items. The tips and practice pages will also help you focus on ways to answer definition questions. So get ready to see a definite improvement in your definition skills!

89

21 Ways to Answer Definition Questions

The key to success on definition tests is studying and memorizing. These 21 study tips will help you get ready for definition tests.

83 Practice a 3-step approach to learning definitions.

Write the words and definitions you want to learn on a sheet of notebook paper. Divide the paper into three vertical sections. Put the word in section one and the definition in section two. Fold section three over section two while you're studying.

84 Use flash cards to study.

Put the word on one side of an index card and its definition on the other side. Use the cards to study by yourself or with a partner.

85 Use a memory strategy for remembering words and definitions.

Use the *Look*, *Say*, and *Write* strategy for learning definitions.

- Look at the word and study the definition.
- Say the word and its definition.
- Write the word.

86 Study words and definitions in groups of five.

Study five words and definitions at a time. After you've learned the first five words and definitions, study another group of five. Then, review all ten words. Continue studying groups of five words and definitions at a time. After studying each group of five, go back and review all the words you've studied before adding any new word groups.

87 Find a study partner.

After you've used the *Look*, *Say*, and *Write* strategy for studying the words, have someone say the words and you give the definitions.

88 Vary the study technique you use with your partner.

You might also want to have someone give you the definitions and you name the words.

21 Ways to Answer Definition Questions, *continued*

89   **Think of short definitions for words.**

Try to think of a one- or two-word definition for a word rather than a long phrase or sentence. For example, instead of memorizing *to accumulate gradually* for the word *gather*, use the word *collect* as your definition.

90   **Highlight prefixes, suffixes, and root words.**

Use colored pens to highlight prefixes, suffixes, and root words. When you learn the meanings of common prefixes, suffixes, and root words, this will help you define words you're unsure of. Look at the example below for the word *preexistence*.

- *Pre* is the prefix. It means *before*.
- *Exist* is the root word. It means *to come into being*.
- *Ence* is the suffix. It means *a state of being*.

By looking at the prefix, suffix, and root word, you can figure out that *preexistence* means *to come into being before something else*.

91   **Learn basic root words.**

Learning root words can help you figure out the meanings of words you're unsure of. For example, the root word *magni*, means *great* or *big*. If you know this, it can help you figure out the meanings of words like *magni*fy, *magni*ficent, and *magni*tude.

92   **Learn prefix meanings.**

Even if you don't know the meaning of the root word, knowing its prefix can give you a clue to the word's meaning. For example, what do you think the word *dissatisfied* means? If you know the prefix *dis* means *not*, you can guess the meaning of this word as *not satisfied*.

93   **Learn suffix meanings.**

Even if you don't know the meaning of the root word, knowing its suffix can give you a clue to the word's meaning. For example, what do you think the word *reliable* means? If you know the suffix *able* means *able to*, you can guess the meaning of this word as *able to rely on*.

21 Ways to Answer Definition Questions, *continued*

94 **Use visualization and association to help recall definitions.**

When you visualize something, you try to picture it in your head. When you associate something, you try to link it to something it's like. For example, you might use visualization and association to remember the meaning of the word *cowl*, which is a monk's hood. To do this, picture the hood coming down in a point over the monk's forehead, like the markings on an owl's face.

95 **Make up jingles to help you learn definitions.**

Making up jingles can help you learn and remember definitions better. For example, you can think of a jingle for the word *separate*, which means *to keep apart*. You might think, "The crowd will sep<u>ara</u>te if a <u>rat</u> appears."

96 **Look for small words within words.**

Long words are often made up of two or three smaller words. Looking for the small words can help you learn to spell the long words. For example, the word *separate* has the words *par* and *ate* in it.

97 **Match your study techniques to the type of test.**

Will the test be a sentence completion test? Will it have a word bank? Will you be asked to take dictation? Will you be asked to provide an antonym or a synonym for a word? Always ask your teacher how the test will be given so you'll know how to study.

98 **Complete the definitions you know first.**

When taking the test, always complete the definitions you know first. Then, you'll know how much time you have left to answer the ones you don't know.

99 **Use the number and length of blanks as a clue to the answer.**

If the definition is given as an incomplete sentence, check the number and length of the blanks. Sometimes this is a clue to the size and the number of words.

100 **Look for "a" or "an" right before the blank.**

If the definition is given as an incomplete sentence, check the word right before the blank. This can be a clue to the word you're looking for. "A" usually comes before a word that starts with a consonant. "An" usually comes before a word that starts with a vowel.

21 Ways to Answer Definition Questions, *continued*

101 **Decide which part of speech is missing from an incomplete sentence.**

If the definition is given as an incomplete sentence, check the part of speech that's missing. Subjects and verbs must agree.   Look at these examples.

> A <u>pilot</u> <u>is</u> the person who flies the plane.
>
> <u>Pilots</u> <u>are</u> people who fly planes.

102 **Use context clues.**

All of the words in a sentence depend on the others.   If you don't know the meaning of a word, look at the words around it for a clue.   This kind of clue is called a *context clue*. There are five types of context clues.

- synonyms
- definition or description
- association
- tone and setting
- cause and effect

103 **Take a chance.**

Ask your teacher if there's a penalty for incorrect answers.   If there isn't a penalty, always guess at definitions you're unsure of.

Prefix and Suffix Meanings

Knowing the meanings of common prefixes and suffixes can help you perform better on definition tests. If you're unsure of the meaning of a word, look to see if it has a prefix or a suffix for a clue. Below are some common prefixes and suffixes and their definitions.

Prefixes	
a, ab - away from	**im** - not
ante - before	**in** - not
anti - against	**inter** - between, among
auto - self	**ir** - not
bi - two	**mis** - wrong
circu - around	**non** - not
co - with, together	**over** - over
counter - against	**pro** - in front, forth
de - away, down	**re** - again
dis - apart from, not	**tele** - far away
ex - from	**trans** - across
extra - outside, beyond	**un** - not
fore - in front	**uni** - one
il - not	**post** - after
sub - under	**super** - over

Suffixes	
able - tending to, able to	**age** - result of
al - relating to	**ance, ence** - state of being
ary, ery - that which	**ive** - given to
en - having nature of, to make	**er** - one who, that which
est - most	**ful** - full of
fy - make or form into	**hood** - state of rank
ist - one who	**ish** - having nature to
less - without	**ly** - in the manner of
ment - action	**most** - most toward
ness - state of being	**or** - person who
ous - state	**ship** - office
tion, ion - act, state	

Context Clues

Context clues are other words in a sentence that tell you about the word you don't know. You can use context clues to help you figure out the meaning of unknown words. There are five kinds of context clues. Look at the examples below.

1. **Synonym**

   A *myth* is a story you don't believe.

   Myth and *story* are synonyms—they mean the same thing.

2. **Definition or Description**

   Maria and Sue are *inseparable* and will never be parted.

   Inseparable is defined as *never parted*.

3. **Association**

   Li is always on time. She double checks her work and can always be counted on in an emergency. Li is a *responsible* worker.

   A *responsible* person is associated with *being on time*, *double checking work*, and *being counted on in an emergency*.

4. **Tone and Setting**

   The sun was intense. The bright, blue sky was clear and the lake shimmered. The scene remains *vivid* in my mind.

   The setting appeared *intense*, *bright*, and *shimmering*. It was *vivid*.

5. **Cause and Effect**

   The suitcase was so small, I had to *compress* my shirts to fit all of them inside.

   If the shirts were *compressed* to fit in a small suitcase, they must have been *flattened* or *squeezed*.

Visual Clues

Name _____

If the definition is given as an incomplete sentence, check the length of the blank. This might be a clue to the size of the word answer.

Use the word bank to complete each sentence below. Don't forget to check the length of the blanks!

match	registration	toothbrush
shelf	encyclopedia	doorknob

1. Articles about different subjects are listed in alphabetical order in an _____.

2. A _____ is a handle that's used to open a door.

3. _____ day is the day you enroll for classes.

4. Things that look good together _____.

5. A _____ is something you use to brush your teeth.

6. A narrow piece of material that's fastened to a wall is called a _____.

Use the word bank to complete each sentence below. Don't forget to check the length of the blanks!

foresight	disk	flower
compliments	echo	dirty

7. The sounds repeated over and over and became an _____.

8. Computer data can be stored on a _____.

9. The water wasn't clean. It was _____.

10. Terri had the _____ to look ahead at tomorrow's weather.

11. A plant cultivated for its blossoms is called a _____.

12. Everyone admired Carlo's new jacket. He received many _____ on it.

Word Clues

Name _____

If the definition is given as an incomplete sentence, check the word right before the blank. If the word is "a," you're probably looking for a word that begins with a consonant. If the word is "an," you're probably looking for a word that begins with a vowel.

Using the word bank, select the correct word for each sentence.

subway	inexpensive	orange
climb	hummingbird	angry

1. A _____ is an underground train.

2. An _____ watch is a cheap watch.

3. An _____ is a citrus fruit.

4. The girl was mad. She had an _____ look on her face.

5. When you _____ the stairs, you go up them.

6. A _____ is a tiny, brightly colored bird with narrow wings.

Using the word bank, select the correct word for each sentence.

candle	twist	annual
insect	frog	illegal

7. A _____ is made of wax and is used to give off light.

8. An _____ has three pairs of legs and one or two pairs of wings.

9. An anniversary is an _____ event.

10. Something that's against the law is _____.

11. To turn is to _____.

12. A _____ has webbed feet, no tail, and leaps.

Subject or Verb?

Name _____

If the definition is given as an incomplete sentence, check the **part of speech** that's missing. Subjects and verbs must agree.

Complete each sentence with the correct word. Make sure the subjects and verbs agree.

minnows	owls	hurricanes
minnow	owl	hurricane

1. The rain, thunder, and strong winds were unbelievable. It was like a _____ had hit our town.

2. _____ are tropical storms with winds of more than 75 miles per hour.

3. A _____ is a live or artificial fish used for bait.

4. _____ are small fish that are less than a designated size.

5. An _____ is a bird that hunts for food at night.

6. _____ are birds with large heads and eyes and short bills.

Complete each sentence with the correct word. Make sure the subjects and verbs agree. You won't use all of the words.

collide	telephones	admire	supervisor
vanishes	airplane	subways	

7. A jet is another name for an _____ .

8. Trains are aboveground railways. _____ are underground railways.

9. I think highly of my grandmother's accomplishments. I _____ her.

10. Snow _____ or disappears when the temperature rises.

11. A _____ is a person who watches over a company's employees.

12. _____ reproduce sounds at a distance for the purpose of **communicating with others**.

What's the Context?

Name _____

Context clues are other words in the sentence that tell you about the word you don't know. Use context clues to complete each sentence below with an appropriate word from the word bank. You won't use all of the words.

stingy	crib	autumn	asleep	encyclopedia
winter	warm	fruit	impatient	police officer
measure	won	angry	hurricane	anniversary

1. The man and woman had been married for ten years. This was their tenth wedding _____ .

2. The man never shared his money. He was very _____ .

3. A _____ is a baby's bed.

4. The fallen leaves were blowing in the cool breeze. We knew that _____ was here.

5. When my sister came home carrying a shiny trophy, I knew her team had _____ the softball tournament.

6. A _____ _____ protects the citizens of a community and enforces the laws set up by the government.

7. We saw snow begin to fall from the sky and knew that _____ was here.

8. The man was so _____ that his face turned red and he began yelling.

9. The coat was so thick and furry that I knew it would keep me _____ .

10. We brought home apples, oranges, and strawberries to make a _____ salad.

11. A _____ is a group of musical notes or beats.

12. The child was so tired that he fell _____ before he took off his clothes.

13. The rain was beating down on the houses and the strong winds sent the waves crashing against the shore. The _____ had hit.

14. Marta's always in a hurry and hates to wait her turn. She's very _____ .

 **Practice Test**

Definition Questions

Place the correct word in the blank in each sentence below. You won't use all of the words.

bait	shake	perennials	tart	unicycle
jack	moist	discouraged	sank	

1. _____ the jar to mix the paint before you use it.

2. Worms, crackers, and minnows can be used for _____ when fishing.

3. A bicycle has two wheels. A _____ has one.

4. Flowers that come up every year are called _____ .

5. The ship went under the sea. It _____ .

6. A small pie is a _____ .

7. A _____ is a tool used to raise a car when changing a tire.

8. The players became _____ , and they lost their confidence after losing their fifth game.

Place the correct word in the blank in each sentence.

eternal	dairy	fun	soaking
painter	fable	aphid	umbrella

9. I thought the game would last forever. It seemed _____ .

10. An _____ is a tiny insect that lives on plants.

11. The children had a good time. They had so much _____ together.

12. Ty stepped off the bus into a big puddle. His boots got _____ wet.

13. A farm dedicated to producing milk, cheese, and butter is called a _____ .

14. A _____ is a person who uses paint and brushes to work.

15. A _____ is a story that has a moral.

16. An _____ is a fabric shade for protection against the weather.

Unit 7: Reading Comprehension Questions

Overview

You can use reading comprehension questions to assess your students' abilities to locate and retrieve information from the printed page. They also allow you to find out about your students' impressions or opinions of what they've read. Finally, reading comprehension questions are a good measure of how well your students can interpret what they read.

Many students become frustrated with reading comprehension questions when they aren't able to easily answer the questions. That's because they often haphazardly search for answers, rather than use a systematic approach to recognizing and understanding important information. The systematic approach presented in this unit is just what your students need to gain success with this format. Student objectives include:

❒ Locating information in passages to answer *who*, *what*, *when*, and *where* questions.

❒ Answering multiple choice questions in response to reading passages.

❒ Determining the main idea of reading passages.

❒ Drawing inferences from reading passages.

❒ Giving personal interpretations or opinions in response to reading passages.

You can help your students perform better on reading comprehension questions by evaluating your method of writing items. The teacher tips below give you information to consider when writing tests.

Teacher Tips for Test Construction

Ask a reasonable number of questions per paragraph. Too many items results in questions that are repetitive or that tap irrelevant information. Too few items results in overlooking important points.

Mix types of items for each paragraph. Ask at least one question for each passage that requires inferential thinking or real-life application.

Avoid introducing new vocabulary words in reading passages. If you do, provide a definition key and type key terms or words in boldface on the test.

Space passages so students have enough room to underline key points and write notes in the margins.

Allow students to use dictionaries during the test, unless your purpose is to assess vocabulary in context.

Focus

Reading Comprehension Questions *(page 104)*

Before introducing the focus, read your students a short magazine or newspaper article. Then, ask them questions about what you read. How well do they remember the facts? Are they able to express their opinions about the article? Explain how being able to identify and remember key points in a reading passage will help your students answer these kinds of questions on a test.

Handout

7 Ways to Answer Reading Comprehension Questions *(page 105)*

This handout gives your students detailed strategies for answering reading comprehension questions. Use it as a springboard for class discussion to familiarize your students with the language of testing. Encourage them to refer to this handout before and during any test that includes reading comprehension questions.

Activity Sheets

Key Points *(page 107)*

Students who have difficulty responding to reading comprehension questions probably haven't identified the key information before attempting to answer the questions. This activity gives your students practice identifying the important points in a reading passage.

Step by Step *(page 108)*

Your students use this strategy to answer multiple choice questions about a reading passage.

- Read the passage twice.
- Circle or underline the key points in the passage.
- Try to answer each question without looking at the choices.
- If you don't know the answer, look at the choices and try to eliminate some of them.
- Look at the passage again to decide which answer to choose.

Main Idea *(page 109)*

Being able to identify the main idea in a passage helps your students stay focused when answering reading comprehension questions. This activity gives them practice naming the main idea in two paragraphs.

What Do You Think? *(pages 110)*

Sometimes you'll want to ask your students to express their opinions about a passage or to give their impressions about some of the information. Through examples and practice items, this activity teaches your students to begin their answers to these kinds of questions by repeating the questions.

Practice Test

Give your students the practice test as a pretest to this unit and as a posttest to assess their progress answering reading comprehension questions. Encourage your students to use the handout from this unit to help them with the posttest.

Focus: Reading Comprehension Questions

Reading comprehension tests ask you to read a passage and respond to it in some way, either by answering questions about it or by giving your impression or opinion of it. You won't be able to study for the exact questions that will be asked on the test, but you can practice finding the important information in a passage.

You should adopt a motto for this unit to remember as you're working on the practice pages. Your motto should be, "Once is not enough!" After quickly reading a passage, go back and read it again. This time look for details and key points. Read it a third time and circle or underline important points. This unit will help you learn how to find important information in reading passages and give you practice thinking about the hidden messages in passages.

7 Ways to Answer
Reading Comprehension Questions

"Once is not enough!" is your motto.   These seven tips tell you more ways you can become a master at answering questions about a reading passage.

104   Read the passage over quickly.

The first time you read through a passage, try to get a general idea of what it's about.

105   Read the passage a second time.

You'll probably be asked questions about the *who, what, where,* and *when* information in the reading passage.   To help you remember this important information, read the passage slowly and carefully the second time.   Circle or underline the names of all the people and places, and the times, dates, and numbers in the passage.   Remember, "Once is not enough!"

106   Try to answer multiple choice questions by looking at the stem only.

Here's a strategy to follow when answering multiple choice questions about a reading passage.

- Read the passage twice.
- Circle or underline the names of all the people and places, and the times, dates, and numbers in the passage.
- Try to answer the question without looking at the choices.
- If you don't know the answer, look at the choices and try to eliminate some of them.
- Look at the passage again to decide which answer to choose.

107   Look back at the passage if you're unsure of the answer.

Not all of the answers to reading comprehension questions can be found in the paragraph, but it's a good place to start if you're unsure of an answer.   Even if the answer isn't stated in the paragraph, looking back at it will remind you of the key points and help you form your answer.

108   Look for the main idea.

The main idea is the most important idea.   It tells you what the paragraph is about.   Some test questions will ask you to read a paragraph and find the main idea.   If a word or phrase isn't used in the passage, or if it's only used once, it's probably not the main idea.

7 Ways to Answer
Reading Comprehension Questions, *continued*

109 **Back up your answer with an explanation or a reason.**

Sometimes you'll be asked to read a passage and tell about your reaction to it or give your opinion. There usually aren't any wrong answers to these types of questions, especially if you back up your answer with a good explanation or reason. Below are some examples of how these kinds of questions start.

"How do you think . . ."

"Why do you think . . ."

"Do you think . . ."

An easy way to begin your answer is to repeat the question.

110 **Double-check your answers.**

You'll get a better grade if you check your answers before handing in your paper. The answers to most reading comprehension questions are somewhere in the reading passage. As you answer each question, look back at the paragraph to make sure you've answered it correctly.

Unit 7: Handout   106

 **Key Points**

Name _____

Quickly read the passage below. Next, read it again slowly, and circle or underline the names of all people and places, and the times, dates, and numbers. Then, answer the questions. The first one is done for you.

<u>Arthur Ashe</u> was a professional tennis player. He was born in Richmond, Virginia, on July 10, 1943. In 1968, he won the U.S. Open and became the United States' top-ranking male tennis player. He turned professional in 1969. Ashe was the first African-American male to win the U.S. Open and Wimbeldon championships. He retired in 1979 after a heart attack and bypass surgery. Sadly, Ashe contracted AIDS from the blood transfusions he received during the surgery, and he died in 1993. He will long be remembered for his humanitarian acts and his many tennis achievements.

1. Who was Arthur Ashe?

   He was a professional tennis player. _____

2. When and where was he born?

   _____

3. What tournament did he win in 1968?

   _____

4. What major tournament did he win in addition to the U.S. Open?

   _____

5. When did he turn professional?

   _____

6. Why did he retire?

   _____

7. What was the cause of his death?

   _____

8. What two achievements will he be remembered for?

   _____

Step by Step

Name _____

Follow these steps to help you answer multiple choice questions about the reading passage below.

- Read the passage twice.
- Circle or underline the key points in the passage.
- Try to answer each question without looking at the choices.
- If you don't know the answer, look at the choices and try to eliminate some of them.
- Look at the passage again to decide which answer to choose.

An *aurora* is a light produced in the upper atmosphere of the earth. Sometimes an aurora looks yellowish-green. Ones that are very high in the atmosphere look red. High auroras may appear violet at twilight.

The aurora that appears in the Northern Hemisphere is called the *aurora borealis*. In the Southern Hemisphere, it's called the *aurora australis*. The most likely places to see an aurora in North America are in Alaska, the Hudson Bay, and Labrador.

1. An aurora is _____ .

   a. a reflection of the earth's oceans

   b. a light produced in the upper atmosphere of the earth

   c. a dense cloud covering the earth's poles.

2. Auroras that are found high in the atmosphere are _____ .

   a. violet at dawn

   b. red

   c. bright green

3. The *aurora borealis* appears in _____ .

   a. the Southern Hemisphere

   b. both hemispheres during the winter months

   c. the Northern Hemisphere

4. If you want to see an aurora in North America, you should go to _____ .

   a   Alaska or Labrador

   b. Ontario

   c. Antarctica

 **Main Idea**

Name _____

The main idea is the most important idea in anything you read. If a word or phrase isn't used in a reading passage, or if it's only used once, it's probably not the main idea. Read each passage. Then, circle the letter of the main idea. The first one is done for you.

1. Hippopotamuses are interesting animals. They live in rivers or lakes in groups of ten to sixty. These groups are called *herds* or *bloats*. Hippopotamuses sleep in the water during the day and graze on grass at night. In Africa, you might see a herd of hippos in the water.

   The main idea of the passage is:

   a. Life in Africa

   b. Hippopotamuses are interesting animals.

   c. A bloat is a group.

2. Hypnosis is a way to help a person focus his awareness. Most people can be hypnotized if their attention can be gained. Hypnosis is used by doctors to study their patients' problems. It's also used to entertain people, like when a magician puts someone in a trance. Some dishonest people claim they can use hypnosis to treat incurable diseases.

   The main idea of the passage is:

   a. Everyone can be hypnotized.

   b. Hypnosis is used for several reasons.

   c. Sleepy people are easy to hypnotize.

   d. Magicians use shiny objects to hypnotize people.

3. Diet books are selling like hotcakes! Some books recommend eating only one kind of food, like vegetables, fish, or fruit. Other books tell people to buy certain diet drinks or meals that cost a lot of money and may not work. Some books even tell people to "think" their extra pounds off by meditating. Only some books tell the true secret to losing weight and staying healthy—eating a balanced, low-fat diet and exercising.

   The main idea of the passage is:

   a. Diet books don't always tell the truth.

   b. Fish helps you lose weight.

   c. You can think about losing weight.

   d. Hotcakes can help people lose weight.

 **What Do You Think?**   Name _____

Not all of the answers to reading comprehension questions can be found in the paragraph. Sometimes you'll be asked to read a passage and tell about your reaction to it or give your opinion. An easy way to begin your answer to these questions is to repeat the question. Look at the examples below.

1. Do you think the citizens will vote for Manny?

   Yes. I think the citizens will vote for Manny because . . .

2. Why do you think Manny wanted to become mayor?

   I think Manny wanted to become mayor because . . . .

3. How do you think Manny's experiences as a police officer helped him win the election?

   I think Manny's experiences as a police officer helped him win the election by . . . .

Now, use the information from each paragraph to help you answer the questions about this reading passage. The first one is done for you.

Shamaro had never traveled more than 25 miles from her home. At age 18, she had an opportunity to attend nursing school with a full scholarship. The only problem was that the school was 500 miles away.

Shamaro had many fears about leaving home, especially for a place so far away. She had always wanted to become a nurse, though, and she knew that her small, rural community desperately needed trained medical professionals.

Most of Shamaro's friends were going to stay at home after graduation to work on family farms or in small businesses. In some ways, Shamaro envied them. However, most of her friends encouraged Shamaro to go out and see the world. This was going to be a very hard decision for Shamaro to make!

1. How do you think Shamaro earned her scholarship?

   I think Shamaro earned her scholarship by getting good grades in school.

110

What Do You Think?, *continued*

2. Why do you think Shamaro had never traveled far from home while she was growing up?

_____

_____

3. What do you think some of her fears were about leaving home?

_____

_____

4. How do you think Shamaro's friends felt about the decision she had to make?

_____

_____

5. How do you think Shamaro would make her decision?

_____

_____

6. What do you think Shamaro decided to do?

_____

_____

7. How do you think Shamaro's friends reacted to her decision?

_____

_____

8. If Shamaro goes to nursing school, do you think she'll return to her community to work as a nurse?

_____

_____

 **Practice Test**

Reading Comprehension Questions

Read the passage and answer the questions.

The brain is divided into two halves that do different tasks. Each half is called a *hemisphere*. The right half of the brain thinks in pictures. It's good at coming up with creative answers to questions or problems.

The left half of the brain thinks in words. It's good at finding answers to specific questions and solving problems. We might say that the left brain is serious and logical, and the right brain is more playful or creative.

Learning is easier when both sides of our brain work together. We use both sides of our brains to do many everyday tasks. For example, when making a cake, we use our left brains to measure the ingredients. We use our right brains to put the layers of the cake together to form a whole and to decorate the cake.

We may use our left brains to memorize history facts, but our right brains help us imagine what it would be like to have lived in another time. Using both sides of our brains helps us balance our view of the world!

Answer the questions.

1. What are the halves of the brain called? _____

2. Which side of the brain is more logical? _____

3. Which side of the brain is more creative? _____

Circle all the choices that are true.

4. The left side of the brain is used to:

    a. balance a checkbook

    b. put a list of words in alphabetical order

    c. finger paint

    d. listen to music

5. The right side of the brain is used to:

    a. memorize state capitals

    b. daydream

    c. choose a new perfume

    d. dial a new telephone number

Practice Test, *continued*

6. Besides baking a cake, name another example of an everyday task in which we use both sides of our brains.

   _____

7. If a person had an accident and injured the left side of his brain, how might this affect his thinking? What kinds of daily activities might he have trouble doing?

   _____

   _____

   _____

   _____

8. The main idea of this passage is:

   a. Artists only use their right brain.

   b. Car accidents cause brain injury.

   c. We should work harder on exercising our brains.

   d. Both sides of the brain are needed to learn and do daily activities.

Unit 8: Essay Questions

Overview

Essay questions are a good way to assess your students' abilities to think critically about a topic, to organize their thoughts logically, and to relate this information in writing. Essay questions also allow your students to apply information and knowledge across different contexts and academic areas.

Some students perform poorly on essay questions because they view them as an opportunity to think and write randomly about a topic, or they don't have the skills to organize their thinking and writing. This unit will show your students that organizing their responses during the prewriting stages is the key to successfully answering essay questions.

This unit provides a sequential model for organizing and answering essay questions, so it's critical that students complete the entire unit in sequence.   Student objectives include:

❏ Locating command words in prompts.

❏ Understanding the meanings of various command words.

❏ Developing topic sentences, main ideas, and details in response to commands.

❏ Using prewriting strategies or graphic organizers in response to commands.

❏ Forming summary statements to close their essays.

❏ Following steps to edit their responses to essay prompts.

You can help your students perform better on essay tests by evaluating your method of writing, grading, and preparing students for essay tests. The teacher tips below give you good information to consider before giving an essay test.

Teacher Tips for Student Success

Underline cue words in prompts.

Provide an adequate amount of space to answer the question.

Give students a choice of items to answer.

Encourage students to use scratch paper to do their prewriting work.

Post tips for editing responses. Remind students to use them during the test.

Ask students to write on lined paper.

Don't penalize students for poor hand-writing. If possible, let students type or tape record answers.

Let students use dictionaries during the test if you're going to deduct points for spelling errors.

Focus

Essay Questions *(page 119)*

Before introducing the focus, talk to your students about some of the fears they have regarding essay questions. Then, discuss some of the advantages to taking essay questions, like being able to express your ideas and share your knowledge. The focus is designed to reassure your students that there's a formula for organizing answers to essay questions that will help reduce anxiety at test time.

Handouts

15 Ways to Answer Essay Questions *(page 120)*

This handout takes your students step-by-step through the process of answering essay questions. Use it as a springboard for class discussion to familiarize your students with the language of testing. Encourage them to refer to this handout before and during any test that includes essay questions.

Command Word Categories *(page 123)*

Command words can be divided into four categories, or purposes. Understanding the meaning and purpose of a command word will help your students formulate their answers to an essay prompt. This handout gives the groupings and meanings of the command words most often found in essay questions. The seven most frequently used command words have been bolded.

Take time to thoroughly discuss the categories and the meanings of the command words with your students. Encourage them to refer to this handout throughout this unit and before and during any test that includes essay questions.

Essay Checklist *(page 125)*

This handout serves as a checklist for students to use when editing their essay responses. You may want to pair students who are having difficulty with students who have a higher level of comprehension when at this stage. Encourage students to ask each other questions about their answers to help them clarify their thinking.

Activity Sheets

Command Words *(page 126)*

Your students need to be able to identify the command word in essay prompts so they know how to answer the question. Emphasize the importance of reading the prompt twice. You may want to discuss the **Command Word Categories** handout on page 123 with your students before beginning this activity.

Counting Commands *(page 127)*

Some essay prompts contain more than one command word. Your students must identify each command word before they begin to write so they don't leave out part of the answer. Allow your students to use the **Command Word Categories** handout on page 123 to complete this activity.

Question Prompts *(page 128)*

When your students are presented with an essay prompt in the form of a question, tell them to change the question into a statement with a command word. Allow them to use the **Command Word Categories** handout on page 123 when forming their statements with command words.

Topic Sentences *(page 129)*

Discuss the importance of a topic sentence with your students. This activity gives them practice restating or paraphrasing the prompt into a topic sentence. They'll use the topic sentences they formed in this activity to complete **Main Points** on page 130, so you may want to collect your students' papers until you're ready to begin that activity.

Main Points *(page 130)*

Have your students use four of the topic sentences they formed when completing **Topic Sentences** on page 129 to practice developing a main idea and details for each sentence.

Describing Organizers *(page 131)*

Your students complete a *Cluster or Word Map* and a *List* graphic organizer for describing prompts.

Your students will use these organizers to complete **Summary Statements** on page 139, so you may want to collect their papers until you're ready to begin that activity.

Outlining or Explaining Organizers *(page 132)*

Your students complete an *Outline* where one or more paragraphs are needed, a *Compare*, a *Contrast*, and a *Compare and Contrast* graphic organizer for outlining or explaining prompts.

Your students will use these organizers to complete **Summary Statements** on page 139, so you may want to collect their papers until you're ready to begin that activity.

Persuading Organizers *(page 136)*

Your students complete a *Least to Most Important Ideas* and a *Pro/Con* graphic organizer for persuading prompts.

Your students will use these organizers to complete **Summary Statements** on page 139, so you may want to collect their papers until you're ready to begin that activity.

Ordering Organizers *(page 138)*

Your students complete a *Sequential* and a *Progression* graphic organizer for ordering prompts.

Your students will use these organizers to complete **Summary Statements** on page 139, so you may want to collect their papers until you're ready to begin that activity.

Summary Statements *(page 139)*

Your students may not realize the impact a good closing statement can add to an essay response. Explain to your students that a summary statement should briefly retell the main idea and details of their essays. Give them examples of phrases that signal closing statements, such as, *In conclusion, To summarize*, and *In closing*.

In this activity, your students practice summarizing their ideas using the strategies they have already learned. Have your students reread the prompts, topic sentences, and details on the graphic organizers they completed on pages 131-138. They'll write summary statements for these prompts.

Write It Out *(page 141)*

Your students are ready to answer an essay question! Have them select two of the graphic organizers from the ones they've developed. Your students use this activity to complete their essays in a written format. Remind them to include a topic sentence, details, and a summary statement in each essay.

To give your students practice managing their time, you may want to set a time limit to complete the second essay.

Practice Test

Because the essay format is difficult for many students, and because of the number of sub-skills involved in developing essay responses, students will benefit from frequent, guided practice answering essay questions. For this reason, a variety of sample essay prompts are provided on the practice test. When you've completed this unit, ask your students to respond to one of the prompts to assess their progress answering essay questions. Encourage them to use the handouts from this unit for help.

Use the additional sample questions for review when your students need to brush up on the skills and sequence used to answer essay prompts.

Focus: Essay Questions

Essay questions give you a great opportunity to show what *you* know and what *you* think about a topic. They give you a chance to think creatively on paper, rather than ask you to come up with what may be only one right answer to a question.

Essay questions make some students nervous because they ask you to fill a blank piece of paper with your own ideas. Other students like essay questions because they don't limit you to narrow choices. Instead, you can express yourself creatively.

Which kind of student are you? If you're one of the students that doesn't like essay questions, this unit is just for you! As you work through the activities in this unit, you'll realize that essay questions are easy to answer once you learn the formula for organizing your answers. Once you complete this unit, you may find that you actually enjoy putting your thoughts down on paper and sharing your knowledge with your teacher.

15 Ways to Answer Essay Questions

There's a step-by-step process to follow when answering essay questions. These 15 tips will lead you down the path to success.

111 Read the prompt.

Essay questions on tests aren't always in the form of questions. They're more like directions that tell you what to do. The direction for an essay question is called a *prompt*. You should read the prompt word-for-word before you begin writing. Don't just skim it over—read every word.

112 Reread the prompt.

Read the prompt a second time to make sure you understand what the direction is asking you to do.

113 Find and underline the command word.

A command word is a verb in an essay prompt that tells you what to do to answer the question. Examples of command words are *list* and *discuss*. You should always identify the command word before you start to write your answer.

Some prompts have more than one command word. Make sure you identify each one before you begin to answer so you don't leave out part of the answer.

114 Define the command word.

What does the command word mean? What are you supposed to do or show in your answer? It's important to know the answers to these questions before you begin writing.

115 Determine the category or purpose of the command word.

There are many possible command words that can be used in essay prompts. They can be divided into four categories to help you decide how to answer a question. These categories tell you the goal you're trying to achieve in your answer. The four categories of command words are:

- describing (you list or name things)
- outlining or explaining (you explain information and give details)
- persuading (you prove, support, or criticize your answer)
- ordering (you put events in the order they happened)

15 Ways to Answer Essay Questions, *continued*

116 Change a question into a statement with a command word.

Some prompts are in the form of questions. If a prompt asks you to answer a question, change the question into a statement with a command word before you begin answering. Here's an example.

> Prompt: What is a natural resource?

> Statement With a Command Word: Define natural resource.

117 Decide if your answer can be completed in one paragraph.

Sometimes you'll need more than one paragraph to answer an essay prompt. If you're not sure, check the number of command words to give you a clue. Generally, you'll need one paragraph for each command word.

118 Form a topic sentence.

The first sentence of your essay is the topic sentence. You may restate the prompt to form your topic sentence. Here's an example.

> Prompt: Discuss your favorite sport.

> Topic Sentence: My favorite sport is football.

119 Write the main idea.

The main idea is the most important idea—it's what you're going to write about in your essay. After you've formed the topic sentence, write the main idea of your essay. Here's an example.

> Topic Sentence: My favorite sport is football.

> Main Idea: Tell why I like football.

120 Add details to your main idea.

Details tell about your main idea. You may list one or more details under your main idea. Here's an example.

> Main Idea: Tell why I like football.

> Detail: I meet new friends.

> Detail: It's good exercise.

> Detail: It's a thinking game.

15 Ways to Answer Essay Questions, *continued*

121   **Use the main idea and details to develop a visual organizer.**

A visual organizer is a chart, outline, list, or word map to follow when writing your answer.   Before you begin writing, use the main idea and details from your outline to develop a visual organizer.   It's important to do this so you organize your ideas on paper before you begin writing your answer.   Here's an example.

122   **Check the time remaining to answer the question.**

Prewriting steps are all the things you do to organize your thoughts before you begin writing out your answer.   Tips **118-121** are the *prewriting steps*.

After you've completed the prewriting steps, check the clock to see how much time you have left to answer the question.   As you're writing, occasionally check the time remaining to answer the question.   You'll want to save enough time to write a summary statement and read through your essay before turning it in.

123   **Complete your answer in a written format.**

Now you're ready to write your answer to the essay prompt.   Follow the information from your prewriting work to write your answer on a separate piece of paper.   Be sure to include the topic sentence and details in your essay.

124   **Close your essay with a summary statement.**

A summary statement is a sentence that briefly retells the main idea and details of your essay.   It may be helpful to begin your summary statement with words that signal closure, like *In conclusion*, *To summarize*, and *In closing*.   Here's an example.

> In closing, I've chosen football as my favorite sport for several reasons—meeting new friends, good exercise, and a mental challenge.

125   **Read your essay to make sure it's complete.**

When you've finished writing, check your answer for the topic sentence, details, and summary statement.   You'll also want to read through your essay to make sure all the sentences are complete, all the words are spelled correctly, and your handwriting is legible.

Command Word Categories

Command words can be divided into four categories that tell their purposes. This handout lists commonly used command words and gives their purposes and meanings.

Describing

Some command words ask you to describe, list, or name things. Below are examples of describing command words and their meanings.

Classify   Group people or things according to category. Then, explain how they go together.

Describe   Write detailed information about the topic. Use details to create a picture for the reader.

Diagram   Use information from the prompt to make a graph, drawing, chart, or organizer. Label all parts and write a brief description of the information presented in the visual.

Identify   Answer *who*, *what*, *when*, *where*, *why*, and *how* about a topic. Keep your answer organized.

Illustrate   Use examples to explain your answer.

Name   Provide a list.

Outlining or Explaining

Some command words ask you to outline or explain information and give details. The following are examples of outlining or explaining command words and their meanings.

Analyze   Tell how the main ideas and details are related and why they're important.

Comment On   Explain or discuss a topic. You could also criticize the topic.

Compare   Tell or show how things are alike.

Contrast   Tell or show how things are different.

Explain   Give a step-by-step explanation of how something works.

Define   Explain what the subject or topic means.

Discuss   Look at an idea or details of an idea. Draw a conclusion based on these details.

Enumerate   Select the main ideas in the prompt and list them one at a time.

Command Word Categories, *continued*

List	Write a specific number of details or reasons. Number them.
Outline	Organize facts and details into main points and sub-points.
Relate	Show how things are connected or related. Tell how one affects the other.
Review	Summarize the important points of a topic.
State	Give your ideas about a topic. Keep your ideas short and to the point.
Summarize	Restate or explain the main points of an idea or topic.

Persuading

Some command words ask you to provide information to prove, support, or criticize your answer. Below are examples of persuading command words and their meanings.

Criticize	Provide the strengths or weaknesses of the topic.
Evaluate	Use your opinion or an expert's opinion to tell why an idea or subject is important. Be sure to present both the good points and the bad points of the idea.
Interpret	Use examples or analogies (related words) to give meaning.
Justify	Give reasons why a topic or idea is important.
Prove	Use facts and details to show that something is true.
Support	State the reasons you agree with a given statement or position, or argue in favor of your own opinion.

Ordering

Some command words ask you to put events in the order they happened. Below are examples of ordering command words and their meanings.

Sequence	Put events in the order that they happened.
Trace	Show the step-by-step progress or history of an idea or event.

Essay Checklist

When you've finished writing, you should read your essay to make sure it's complete. Use the checklist below to edit your work.

Check one

Yes   No

_____ _____   I began with a topic sentence.

_____ _____   I provided details to support the topic sentence.

_____ _____   I finished with a summary statement.

_____ _____   All my sentences are complete.

_____ _____   My handwriting is legible.

_____ _____   My spelling is correct.

If you checked *Yes* to all of the statements, you've mastered the steps in writing a good essay response!

Command Words

Name _____

A command word is a verb in an essay prompt that tells you what to do to answer the question. It's important to identify the command word before you begin writing your answer.

Find the command word in each prompt below and underline it. The first one is done for you.

1. <u>Discuss</u> your favorite sport.

2. List the steps in building a bonfire.

3. Explain how to bake a cake.

4. Compare fruits and vegetables.

5. Contrast a bicycle and a motorcycle.

6. Compare and contrast a bicycle and a motorcycle.

7. Support your reasons for liking school.

8. Evaluate this statement: Summer is the best season of the year.

9. Trace the steps in getting a driver's license.

10. Comment on the need for children to wear bicycle helmets.

Counting Commands

Name _____

Some prompts have more than one command word. Make sure you identify each one before you begin to answer so you don't leave out part of the answer.

Read each prompt below. Find the command words and underline them. The first one is done for you.

1. <u>List</u> the characteristics of a good movie and <u>select</u> the two that are the most important to you.

2. Summarize the plot and state the main theme of the short story.

3. Review the steps in making bread and list the ingredients.

4. Relate nutrition to health. Tell how good nutrition can help keep you healthy.

5. Trace the steps that tell how a caterpillar becomes a butterfly. Identify things that might interfere with each stage.

6. Comment on the problem of litter on our highways. State your ideas about controlling litter.

7. Describe the process of making paper. Comment on how recycled paper can be used in the process.

8. Discuss the use of pesticides and its effect on wildlife. Propose an alternative to pesticide use.

9. Compare typewriters to word processors. Identify at least two advantages of each.

10. List the main events in the order they occurred in the story. Name the characters that were involved in each event. Identify the place that each event occurred.

11. Criticize this statement: Modern art isn't real art—it's simply colors and designs on canvas.

12. Analyze the writer's argument in this editorial. State whether you agree or disagree with her. Justify the right of the author to send this editorial to the newspaper.

Question Prompts

Name _____

The prompts below are in the form of questions. Change each question into a statement with a command word. The first one is done for you.

1. What's the best material for making a tent? Why?

   Discuss the best material for making a tent. _____

2. What are three objects that come from the soil and how do people use them?

   _____

   _____

3. What are the main causes of fires in homes? What can people do to prevent them?

   _____

   _____

4. How is a person's lifestyle related to how long he or she might live?

   _____

   _____

5. What are the main differences between compact disc players and cassette tape players?

   _____

   _____

6. In your opinion, what are the three biggest problems facing teenagers today? Why?

   _____

   _____

7. How are the United States and Canada alike and different?

   _____

   _____

 **Topic Sentences**   Name _____

The first sentence of your essay is the topic sentence. You may restate the prompt to form your topic sentence. Rewrite each prompt below into a topic sentence. The first one is done for you.

1. Discuss your favorite sport.

   My favorite sport is football. _____

2. List the steps in building a bonfire.

   _____

3. Explain how to bake a cake.

   _____

4. Compare fruits and vegetables.

   _____

5. Contrast a bicycle and a motorcycle.

   _____

6. Compare and contrast a bicycle and a motorcycle.

   _____

7. Support your reasons for liking school.

   _____

8. Evaluate this statement: Summer is the best season of the year.

   _____

9. Trace the steps in getting a driver's license.

   _____

10. Comment on the need for children to wear bicycle helmets.

   _____

 **Main Points**

Name _____

The main idea is the most important idea—it's what you're going to write about in your essay. Details tell about the main idea.

Write a main idea and details for four of the topic sentences you've already formed. An example is done for you.

       Topic Sentence: *My favorite sport is football.* _____

           Main Idea: *Tell why I like football.* _____

               Detail: *I meet new friends.* _____

               Detail: *It's good exercise.* _____

               Detail: *It's a thinking game.* _____

1. Topic Sentence: _____

    Main Idea: _____

       Detail: _____

       Detail: _____

       Detail: _____

2. Topic Sentence: _____

    Main Idea: _____

       Detail: _____

       Detail _____

       Detail: _____

3. Topic Sentence: _____

    Main Idea: _____

       Detail: _____

       Detail: _____

       Detail: _____

4. Topic Sentence: _____

    Main Idea: _____

       Detail: _____

       Detail: _____

       Detail: _____

Describing Organizers   Name _____

It's important to organize your ideas on paper before writing out your answer. To do this, use the main idea and details from your outline to develop a visual organizer.

Study the describing visual organizers. The prompts and topic sentences are given. Some of the main ideas and details are given. First, fill in the missing main ideas and details. Then, use them to complete each organizer.

1. **Prompt: Discuss your favorite sport.**

   Topic Sentence: My favorite sport is football.

   Main Idea: Tell why I like football.

   Detail: I meet new friends.

   Detail: It's good exercise.

   Detail: It's a thinking game.

Organizer Type: Cluster or Word Map

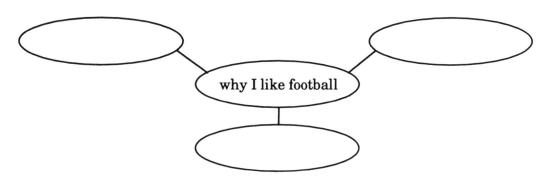

why I like football

2. **Prompt: List the steps in building a bonfire.**

   Topic Sentence: It's easy to build a bonfire.

   Main Idea: There are several steps involved.

   Detail: Find a dry, open area.

   Detail: Collect twigs and branches.

   Detail: _____

Organizer Type: List

   1.   Find a dry, open area.

   2.   _____

   3.   _____

Outlining
or Explaining Organizers

Name _____

It's important to organize your ideas on paper before writing out your answer. To do this, use the main idea and details from your outline to develop a visual organizer.

Study the outlining or explaining visual organizers. The prompts and topic sentences are given. Some of the main ideas and details are given. First, fill in the missing main ideas and details. Then, use them to complete each organizer.

1. **Prompt: Explain how to bake a cake.**

Topic Sentence:	Anyone can bake a cake if he follows the directions.
Main Idea:	Get everything ready before you begin.
Detail:	Find a recipe.
Detail:	Get out the ingredients.
Detail:	_____
Main Idea:	Follow the directions carefully.
Detail:	_____
Detail:	_____
Detail:	_____

Organizer Type: Outline

I. Get everything ready before you begin.

   A. Find a recipe.

   B. _____

   C. _____

II. Follow the directions carefully.

   A. _____

   B. _____

   C. _____

Outlining or Explaining Organizers, *continued*

You can also use these organizers for an outline format.

more than one paragraph

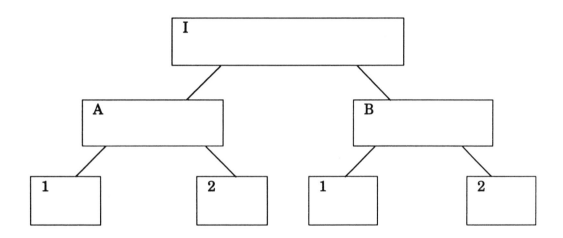

one paragraph

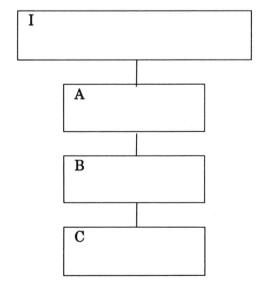

Outlining or Explaining Organizers, *continued*

2. **Prompt: Compare fruits and vegetables.**

   Topic Sentence: Fruits and vegetables are alike in many ways.

   Main Idea: They have many characteristics in common.

   Detail: They're good for you.

   Detail: _____

   Detail: _____

Organizer Type: Compare

    fruits   vegetables

good for you

_____

_____

3. **Prompt: Contrast a bicycle and a motorcycle.**

   Topic Sentence: Bicycles and motorcycles are different in several ways.

   Main Idea: They look alike but are really very different.

   Detail: Bicycles are quiet and motorcycles are noisy.

   Detail: _____

   Detail: _____

Organizer Type: Contrast

    bicycles   motorcycles

    quiet   noisy

_____   _____

_____   _____

Outlining or Explaining Organizers, *continued*

4. **Prompt: Compare and contrast a bicycle and a motorcycle.**

Topic Sentence: Bicycles and motorcycles are alike and different in many ways.

Main Idea: _____

Detail: They both have two wheels.

Detail: _____

Detail: _____

Main Idea: _____

Detail: Bicycles are quiet and motorcycles are noisy.

Detail: _____

Detail: _____

Organizer Type: Compare and Contrast

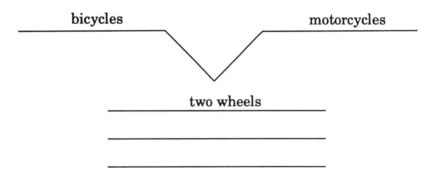

Compare

bicycles   motorcycles

two wheels
_____
_____

Contrast

bicycles   motorcycles

quiet   noisy
_____   _____
_____   _____

Persuading Organizers   Name _____

It's important to organize your ideas on paper before writing out your answer. To do this, use the main idea and details from your outline to develop a visual organizer.

Study the persuading visual organizers. The prompts and topic sentences are given. Some of the main ideas and details are given. First, fill in the missing main ideas and details. Then, use them to complete each organizer.

1. **Prompt: Support your reasons for liking school.**

      Topic Sentence: There are four reasons why I like school.

          Main Idea: _____

               Detail: _____

               Detail: _____

               Detail: _____

               Detail: It's a chance to see my friends.

Organizer Type: Least to Most Important Ideas

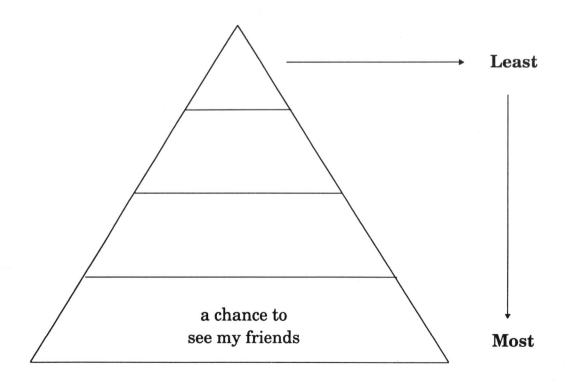

Persuading Organizers, *continued*

2. **Prompt: Evaluate this statement: Summer is the best season of the year.**

Topic Sentence: I disagree with the statement that summer is the best season.

Main Idea: _____

Detail: _____

Detail: _____

Detail: _____

Organizer Type: Pro (for) and Con (against)

Tip: If a prompt asks you to choose a side, develop a brainstorming list. Organize your points from least to most important. The longest side is probably the side you can support the best.

Pro (for)	Con (against)
1. The days are longer.	1. The temperature is hot.
2. _____	2. _____
3. _____	3. _____
4. _____	4. _____
5. _____	5. _____
6. _____	6. _____

Ordering Organizers

Name _____

It's important to organize your ideas on paper before writing out your answer. To do this, use the main idea and details from your outline to develop a visual organizer.

Study the ordering visual organizers. The prompts and topic sentences are given. Some of the main ideas and details are given. First, fill in the missing main ideas and details. Then, use them to complete each organizer.

1. **Prompt: Trace the steps in getting a driver's license.**

   Topic Sentence: There are five steps in getting a driver's license.

   Main Idea: The steps must be followed in order.

   Detail: You must first study for a learner's permit.

   Detail: _____

   Detail: _____

   Detail: _____

   Detail: _____

Organizer Type: Sequential

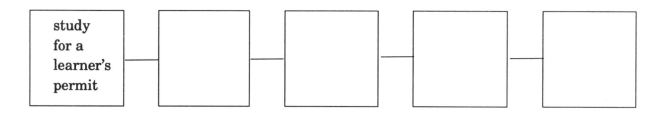

2. **Prompt: Comment on the need for children to wear bicycle helmets.**

   Topic Sentence: There are several important reasons why children need to wear bicycle helmets.

   Main Idea: _____

Organizer Type: Progression

   Reason 1:   Many children have bicycle accidents.

   Reason 2:   _____

   Reason 3:   _____

 **Summary Statements**   Name _____

A summary statement is a sentence that briefly retells the main idea and details of your essay. You should begin your summary statement with words that signal closure, like *In conclusion*, *To summarize*, and *In closing*.

Reread the prompts, topic sentences, and details in your completed graphic organizers. Then, write a summary statement for each of the prompts below. The first one is done for you.

1. Discuss your favorite sport.

   In closing, I have chosen football as my favorite sport for several reasons—meeting

   new friends, good exercise, and a mental challenge.

2. List the steps in building a bonfire.

   _____

   _____

3. Explain how to bake a cake.

   _____

   _____

4. Compare fruits and vegetables.

   _____

   _____

5. Contrast a bicycle and a motorcycle.

   _____

   _____

6. Compare and contrast a bicycle and a motorcycle.

   _____

   _____

Summary Statements, *continued*

7. Support your reasons for liking school.

   _____

   _____

8. Evaluate this statement: Summer is the best season of the year.

   _____

   _____

9. Trace the steps in getting a driver's license.

   _____

   _____

10. Comment on the need for children to wear bicycle helmets.

    _____

    _____

 **Write It Out**

Name _____

After you've finished your visual organizer, you can complete your answer in writing. Use two of the graphic organizers you've already developed to write two paragraphs. Be sure to include a topic sentence, details, and a summary statement in each essay.

_____

_____

_____

_____

_____

_____

_____

_____

_____

_____

_____

_____

_____

_____

 **Practice Test**

Name _____

Essay Questions

1. Describe your favorite foods.

2. Classify the subjects taught in our school by the amount of homework.

3. Contrast an elementary school with a high school.

4. Criticize this statement: All vehicles on interstate highways should be allowed to drive 70 miles an hour.

5. Define the concept of freedom.

6. Compare and contrast two of your favorite sports.

7. Comment on the practice of putting stray animals to sleep.

8. Illustrate the principle of camouflage for survival among insects and animals.

9. Name the six most influential public figures over the last decade.

10. State your viewpoint on the right and responsibility of all citizens to vote.

11. Explain how you would govern if you were elected the leader of your country.

12. Interpret the saying: All's well that ends well.

13. Identify the main characters and events of your favorite novel.

14 Support this observation with facts: High school students are under more stress today than they were 25 years ago.

15. Evaluate the proposal that students must receive a **C** or better in all subjects to participate in extracurricular activities.

16. Trace your family for three generations (your grandparents, your parents, you and your brothers and sisters). Tell something special about each generation.

17. Justify a proposed ban on all disposable soft drink containers.

18. Outline the steps you would take in purchasing a used car.

19. Review the five most significant national or international events that have occurred in your lifetime.

20. Prove this statement: It's always earlier in California than in New York.

21. Review the important events in the history of rock and roll since 1950.

22. Classify each of the professional sports as either a group sport or an individual sport.

23. Analyze the plot of your favorite movie.

24. Discuss how the roles of husbands and fathers have changed over the last 20 years.

25. Relate the enthusiasm of a teacher to the students' levels of participation and achievement.

ANSWER KEY

General Test-Taking Skills

Key Words and Phrases, p.20
1. circle the letter
2. choose the best answer
3. fill in each blank
4. finish each sentence
5. put a *T* next to each statement
6. draw a circle around
7. list the colors
8. circle the word *False*
9. answer three questions
10. choose the letter, write it on the line
11. choose the word, write it in the blank
12. cross out the incorrect term
13. match each definition with a word
14. develop a paragraph or two

Know Your Stuff, p. 21
answers will vary

Cross It Out, p. 22
1. define each word
2. don't leave out any events
3. after reading the passage
4. write a word in the blank to complete each sentence
5. match each event with its date
6. Below are ten definitions. Place the letter of the correct term in the space next to its definition
7. The map below shows the average annual rainfall in South America. You may write on the map.
8. For each statement below . . . based on your knowledge of the word in italics . . . . Indicate your choice.
9. Be sure to write your answers in the form of questions rather than statements.
10. Be sure the sentence shows the meaning of the word in context.

Practice Test, p. 23
1. a
2. b
3. c
4. a
5. a. good
   b. bad
   c. bad
   d. good
   e. good
   f. bad

True/False

Cue Words, p. 32
1. usually
2. many
3. sometimes
4. most
5. worst
6. never
7. some
8. many
9. seldom
10. not
11. invariably
12. all
13. some
14. always
15. worst

Cue Word Clues, p. 33
all answers are false
1. all
2. never
3. worst
4. none
5. only
6. always
7. exactly
8. totally
9. not
10. always
11. every
12. invariably
13. only
14. best

More Cue Word Clues, p. 34
all answers are true
1. many
2. generally
3. probably
4. often
5. more
6. usually
7. frequently
8. mainly
9. seldom
10. often
11. sometimes
12. occasionally
13. might

It's an Exception, p. 35
answers will vary

All or None, p. 36
1. lazy
2. bicycles
3. Minnesota
4. seven
5. Australia
6. cinnamon
7. covered with fur
8. live in the water
9. Texas
10. citrus fruit
11. born in the U.S.
12. stronger bones

Negative to Positive, p. 37
1. don't/won't, true
2. not/will not, true
3. don't/will not, false
4. cannot/do not, true
5. shouldn't/cannot, true
6. don't/will not, false
7. does not/will not, true
8. don't/won't, false
9. don't/won't, true

Word Play, p. 38
1. True, never
2. False, not
3. False, inactive
4. False, impolite
5. False, never improve
6. False, incomplete
7. True, unable
8. False, incurable
9. False, irresponsible
10. False, unlikely
11. False, never impatient
12. False, not
13. False, improper
14. False, disapprove
15. False, never
16. False, impossible

Practice Test, p. 39
1. False
2. False
3. True
4. True
5. False
6. True
7. False
8. False
9. True
10. True
11. False
12. True
13. False
14. True
15. False
16. True
17. True
18. False
19. True
20. False
21. False
22. True
23. True
24. True
25. False

Multiple Choice

What's the Direction?, p. 49
1. correct
2. best
3. correct
4. correct
5. best
6. correct
7. best
8. best
9. correct
10. correct
11. best
12. correct
13. correct
14. best

Multiple Parts, p. 50
students label stems and choices

Question Type, p. 51
1. IS
2. Q
3. IS
4. Q
5. IS
6. Q

Key Words, p. 52
1. cannot
2. except
3. incorrectly
4. not
5. only, not
6. except
7. false
8. incorrect
9. not
10. cannot
11. except
12. false

Attempt An Answer, p. 53
1. c
2. a
3. b
4. c
5. b
6. a
7. b
8. d

Does It Make Sense?, p. 54
1. a
2. a
3. c
4. a
5. c
6. d
7. b
8. a

Distractors!, p. 55
1. C
2. A
3. D
4. B
5. B

Practice Test, p. 56
1. B
2. D
3. C
4. D
5. A
6. C
7. B
8. C
9. A
10. C

Answer Key   144   Copyright © 1994 LinguiSystems, Inc.

Matching

Is It Clear?, p. 64
1. C, A, B, D
2. C, A, B, D
3. 3, 1, 2, 4

How Many Choices, p. 65
1. C
2. A
3. B
4. C
5. D
6. B
7. G
8. E
9. F
10. D
11. E
12. A
13. B
14. C
15. G

Starting Point, p. 66
1. B
2. D
3. A
4. E
5. G
6. C
7. d
8. f
9. a
10. e
11. b
12. c

Speech Parts, p. 67
1. B
2. A
3. C
4. B
5. A
6. C
7. B
8. C
9. A
10. B
11. A
12. C
13. C
14. A
15. B

Matching Mania, p. 68
1. B, C, A, D
2. g, b, c, e, f, a

Practice Test, p. 69
1. C
2. A
3. G
4. F
5. B
6. D
7. D
8. F
9. G
10. A
11. B
12. E

Completion

Which Do You Know?, p. 77
1. eagle
2. ribbons
3. red
4. poison
5. help
6. flag
7. married
8. crime
9. boy
10. school
11. birthday
12. choking

Answer Clues, p. 78
1. instrument
2. season
3. octopus
4. umbrella
5. rainbow
6. bee
7. earring
8. menu
9. escalator
10. uncle
11. sling
12. palm

Grammar Clues, p. 79
1. children
2. adult
3. birds
4. ostrich
5. covers
6. leak
7. measures
8. measure
9. planets
10. revolves
11. studies
12. study

Long or Short?, p. 80
1. car
2. ship
3. airplane
4. motorcycle
5. bicycles
6. buses
7. train
8. buggy
9. helicopter
10. submarine
11. sailboat
12. subway

Count 'Em!, p. 81
1. Dagwood
2. Charlie Brown
3. Casper
4. Mickey Mouse
5. Batman
6. Dennis the Menace
7. Barney Rubble
8. Bugs Bunny
9. Garfield
10. Popeye
11. Road Runner
12. Snow White

On Your Own, p. 82
1. saliva
2. muscles
3. heart
4. liver
5. nerves
6. blood
7. gall bladder
8. immune system
9. teeth
10. tonsils

Unused Words, p. 83
1. illness
2. six
3. healthy
4. fat
5. seat belts
6. twice
7. walking
8. physical
9. cigarettes
10. stretch
11. milk
12. antibiotics

Part and Whole, p. 84
1. digestion, mouth, tongue, teeth, salivary glands
2. cigarettes, cancer, diet, vegetables, environment, loud noise, pollution

Practice Test, p. 85
1. five senses
2. microscope
3. hypothesis
4. data
5. classifying
6. scientific method
7. citizen
8. alien
9. immigrant
10. passport
11. illegal alien
12. exam

Definition

Visual Clues, p. 96
1. encyclopedia
2. doorknob
3. registration
4. match
5. toothbrush
6. shelf
7. echo
8. disk
9. dirty
10. foresight
11. flower
12. compliments

Word Clues, p. 97
1. subway
2. inexpensive
3. orange
4. angry
5. climb
6. hummingbird
7. candle

8. insect
9. annual
10. illegal
11. twist
12. frog

Subject or Verb?, p. 98
1. hurricane
2. hurricanes
3. minnow
4. minnows
5. owl
6. owls
7. airplane
8. subways
9. admire
10. vanishes
11. supervisor
12. telephones

What's the Context?, p. 99
1. anniversary
2. stingy
3. crib
4. autumn
5. won
6. police officer
7. winter
8. angry
9. warm
10. fruit
11. measure
12. asleep
13. hurricane
14. impatient

Practice Test, p. 100
1. shake
2. bait
3. unicycle
4. perennials
5. sank
6. tart
7. jack
8. discouraged
9. eternal
10. aphid
11. fun
12. soaking
13. dairy
14. painter
15. fable
16. umbrella

Reading Comprehension

Key Points, p. 107
1. a professional tennis player
2. Richmond, Virginia July 10, 1943
3. the 1968 U.S. Open
4. Wimbeldon
5. 1969
6. heart attack and bypass surgery
7. AIDS
8. humanitarian acts and tennis achievements

ANSWER KEY

Step by Step, p. 108
1. b
2. b
3. c
4. a

Main Idea, p. 109
1. b
2. b
3. a

What Do You Think?, p. 110
answers will vary

Practice Test, p. 112
1. right
2. left
3. right
4. a, b
5. b, c
6. answers will vary
7. answers will vary
8. d

Essay

Command Words, p. 126
1. discuss
2. list
3. explain
4. compare
5. contrast
6. compare and contrast
7. support
8. evaluate
9. trace
10. comment

Counting Commands, p. 127
1. list, select
2. summarize, state
3. review, list
4. relate, tell
5. trace, identify
6. comment, state
7. describe, comment
8. discuss, propose
9. compare, identify
10. list, name, identify
11. criticize
12. analyze, state, justify

Questions Prompts, p. 128
1. Discuss the best material for making a tent.
2. List three objects that come from the soil and describe how people use them.
3. State the main causes of fires in homes and list ways people can prevent them.
4. Relate a person's lifestyle to his or her life span.
5. Contrast a compact disc player and a cassette player.
6. Comment on the three biggest problems facing teenagers today.
7. Compare and contrast the United States and Canada.

Topic Sentences, p. 129
answers will vary

Main Points, p. 130
answers will vary

Describing Organizers, p. 131
answers will vary

Outlining or Explaining Organizers, p. 132
answers will vary

Persuading Organizers, p. 136
answers will vary

Ordering Organizers, p. 138
answers will vary

Summary Statements, p. 139
answers will vary

Write It Out, p. 141
answers will vary

Practice Test, p. 142
answers will vary

Appendix: Tips for Better Testing Results

Creating Successful Test Formats

There are many ways of assessing student mastery of skills and subject matter. A written test is only one way, and it may not be the best. Below are some alternative testing methods for you to consider.

- ❏ class presentations
- ❏ demonstrations
- ❏ small group discussions
- ❏ individual interviews
- ❏ projects
- ❏ work samples

If you decide a written test is the best means of assessment, you'll want to think carefully about the design of the test. Test format can be an important element in encouraging student success. Appearance, length, and item selection can all affect how your students perform. Here are some ways to improve test formats.

Leave plenty of "white space" on tests. Too much print on a test page can overwhelm students, particularly if they have trouble visually discriminating among test items. Space constraints may also restrict your students' ability to answer open-ended questions.

Type your tests. Handwritten tests can confuse students with visual processing problems. Typed test items are easier to read and answer. They also reinforce the importance of the test.

Make clear, dark copies, using black dittoes or the copy machine.

Avoid making the test longer than is needed to assess the major concepts, and make sure it can be completed without difficulty in the time allotted. Tests with too many questions or pages may encourage students with a history of poor test performance or test anxiety to give up before they even begin. Tests of reasonable length are easier on you and your students.

Match the test item type to the material covered in class and the way the material was taught. If you've stressed details, true/false, matching, or multiple choice items may tap the students' understanding of this material better than short answer or essay questions.

Use at least two question item types on each test. Different students do better on different types of items. A mixture of question types gives all students a chance of success.

Be careful when using unit tests that accompany published materials. Many times these tests don't correspond with the way information was taught in class. For example, vocabulary definitions on published tests may vary from the definitions you presented in class. These differences will confuse some students.

Grading Tests

The way you grade tests can be part of the learning process for your students. Consider adding the tips below to your grading process.

Look over the test with each student when it's turned in. Point out any items she needs to review or reconsider before turning in the test.

Avoid penalizing students for following directions incorrectly. The purpose of testing is to assess knowledge and progress.

Give partial credit whenever possible. Learning is a sequential process, and a test assesses where a student is in the process.

If you err in grading, err in favor of the student. If you know the student had the right answer in mind, consider giving him partial credit, even though the answer isn't correctly stated. Another option would be to allow the student to verbally justify his answer.

Encourage students to challenge your grading. A student will often demonstrate more knowledge in verbally defending her answer than in writing it.

If you make a mistake in grading by marking an incorrect answer correct, let the student keep those points. This encourages an open atmosphere and sets an example for appropriate behavior in accounting for one's mistakes.

Mark papers positively. For example, write +82, rather than -18. Write positive phrases, exclamation points, checks, or pluses in the margins next to answers.

Respect your students' feelings and their right to privacy concerning their grades. Mark grades at the bottom of the last test page, fold papers when returning them, or write "see me" instead of a grade on failing papers. You may want to reconsider when asking students to exchange papers for grading.

Throw out an item if 75% or more of the class misses it. The item may not represent what was taught in class, or it may need to be rewritten.

Following-Up On Tests

Poor test scores need not mark an end of the learning process. Here are some ways you can work with students who have poor test scores.

Look for patterns of error in a student's approach to taking tests that reflect poor test-taking skills. Point these out to the student and work with him on developing these skills.

If a student fails a test or scores poorly, provide an opportunity for her to make up some of the missing points. A retest for partial credit or some other means of assessment might be considered.

If you're aware that a student has particular difficulty with testing, allow him to verbally review his test with you before you grade it. As the student explains each answer, grade it, giving credit for knowledge the student has mastered but not shown on the test.

Adapting Tests for Students With Test-Taking Problems

Simple adaptations in test design can help many students who have difficulty with test taking. Here are some suggestions for adaptations.

Use the same format from one test to the next. Pay special attention to the placement of answer choices, the response mode, and the wording of directions.

Use large type, leave plenty of white space on the page, and draw bold lines between sections.

Use highlighters to identify key words in directions or entire direction statements.

Encourage students to use dark paper as a guide for underlining the items they're working on.

Provide a completed example of each type of question on the test.

Avoid having students transfer answers to a separate answer sheet.

Use only one type of item per page. If a student is taking a test apart from a group, give her one section at a time. This will prevent the student from feeling overwhelmed by the length of the test or from becoming confused by different directions.

Change short answer questions or listing items to multiple choice, true/false, or matching in order to provide response clues.

Read the questions aloud to the student if reading is a barrier in assessing the student's knowledge.

Allow the student to use a tape recorder or a word processor to record his answers.

Encourage answers that are in the student's own words, rather than expecting a repeat of your words or those in the text.

Provide a shortened version of the test, if necessary. Split the test in half (split-half technique) or star important items and ask students to respond to those items only.

References

Millman, J., C.H. Bishop, and R. Ebel. "Analysis of Test-wiseness." *Educational and Psychological Measurement*, Vol. 25, 1965, pp. 707-726.

Scruggs, T.E. and M.A. Mastropieri. *Teaching Test-Taking Skills*. Cambridge, MA: Brookline Books, 1992.

Sebranek, P. *The Write Source*. Burlington, WI: Write Source Educational Publishing House, 1987.

Strichart, S.S. and C.T. Mangrum. *Teaching Study Strategies to Students with Learning Disabilities*. Boston, MA: Allyn and Bacon, 1993.

Wood, J.W. *Adapting Instruction for Mainstreamed and At-Risk Students*. Columbus, OH: Macmillan Publishing Company, 1992.

1-4-234567